# Calm beyond the Reef
# of
# Self-doubts

## A Christian Testimony

Caroline Webb

BALBOA.
PRESS

A DIVISION OF HAY HOUSE

Scripture quotations are from the
Contemporary English Version. (CEV)
(c)American Bible Society 1991, 1995.

Balboa Press books may be ordered through booksellers or by contacting:

Balboa Press
A Division of Hay House
1663 Liberty Drive
Bloomington, IN 47403
www.balboapress.com
1 (877) 407-4847

Printed in the United States of America.

ISBN: 978-1-4525-2752-9 (sc)
ISBN: 978-1-4525-2753-6 (e)

Balboa Press rev. date: 02/02/2015

# FOREWORD

I would like to say this loving gentle lady shows the love of Christ in everything she does.
Her total demeanour throughout this book shows her Christian faith, she has at all times put
the Father in Heaven first, even when going through as said 'the tough times' she has written
with love in her heart, for all those walking beside her, and certainly for those against her.
I am blessed and very honoured to be a dear friend and, to know her as I do.
The words of wisdom and her knowledge of the Christian life are available for all of us, and
written on the pages of this remarkable story.
This book is a story of her walk to and, with Jesus Christ, leading her to be where she is
now, in total peace.
Dorothy McKeown

# FROM THE AUTHOR

Although I have written a story of my life, when it comes to where I am now although still in truth there is a difference. For it is the present, I am to fulfil the future.

I get up in the morning, spend time on my computer compiling more Christian works, or whatever comes into my heart, I love cooking and dogs. And I own two gorgeous very spoilt terriers. One might say terrors.

The kitchen and my desk are where you may find me, I am not a social person, I like being at home for it is my domain.

I am living the farm life still and so very happy with my new farmer husband.

We have similar interests for he is a Christian Believer and this has us involved with our church life. We are on the local Parish Council.

I take church services if needed, and have volunteered to do the same at Rest Homes for the elderly.

The privilege of working with and for God makes my present life a bonus.

This does not take away the fact I am human and can spend moments in a day being 'Very Human'!

My now, marriage has blessed me with an extended family, which in itself is interesting, for we are now a family of eight.

My heart is light for I have taken upon myself the scripture from

**Matthew11:28-29** (CEV). Jesus speaking,

*If you are tired from carrying heavy burdens, come to me and I will give you rest.*

*Take the yoke I give you. Put it on your shoulders and learn from me. I am gentle and humble, and you will find rest. This yoke is easy to bear and this burden is light.*

# DEDICATION

*I want to dedicate this story to my parents, my sister and to my husband who are now all deceased.*

*My life now is not centred on the past, although I do have precious memories.*

*With the quiet guidance of the Lord Jesus, I have met and married again, a beautiful man who is a Believing Believer like me.*

*To God be the Glory. Amen*

*I also dedicate this writing, to the many going through a crisis in their lives. I would like to give special mention to those who have come to me through the gentle guidance of the Holy Spirit, the first Cross Bearer, and to those who have quietly and gently, and not so quietly and gently, stood beside me as I grew with God, and have witnessed my coming to where I am now.*

*IN THE FULL LIGHT OF "JESUS". The Word of Truth, for He says He is the Word, the Truth and the Way.*

*What happens to us on our journey through life is not what God watches; it is our reactions. We as Believing Believers were given at the Cross the power to be over comers.*

*By surrendering myself to God in totality, I am able to step out with confidence wherever I am led, to proclaim the 'living word'.*

*For I live to say,*

*'Thy will be done.'*

*Hallelujah*

# PRELUDE

There was a very sad unhappy woman who carried a myriad of mixed emotions in her heart; they were turning her into a shadow of her real self.

Her bitterness, she carried like a banner hoping they were seen, but not herself, the mask on her face was several layers thick for she wanted to hide not her emotions, but herself, she didn't want to see anyone.

One day when asked if she would like to go to a Christian Fellowship meeting in a nearby town, her reply was 'I have nothing to do so, okay', immediately the words were out of her mouth she felt ill, for fellowship meant people.

In due course the day arrived for this outing, and off two women went one happy and talkative, the other resentful and dull.

The hall suddenly appeared and both, went inside to be met with happy chatter and smiling faces. The bile coming up into the mouth of the unhappy woman was to say the least very unpleasant; she was hoping it could be removed some way without spewing out of her mouth. She didn't want the embarrassment of being noticed.

Everyone was seated, and the meeting started, there was an air of expectancy, all were looking eagerly at the speaker.

This is except the unhappy woman, who had gone into a world of her own bitterness, where no one could reach her or so she thought.

While she sat in this room full of smiling women, a feeling of peace started, to enfold her, it was warm and comforting.

She was reminiscing on some of the events in her past, paying no attention to the message being delivered in front of her, until the words 'Here I am' made her aware of where she was, and the speaker in front.

Suddenly the woman came out of her reverie, and almost physically fell to attention, the simplicity of the words 'Here I am' had somehow caught her attention and as she started to listen she opened her Bible at the book

**_Samuel 3:4.(CEV)_** someone was calling Samuel, the speaker and the Bible; both say 'it was God'.

The speaker was very confident in her delivery, she believed what she was saying, and as the woman listened a soft calm came over her and she found she believed as well.

As she went on this biblical path with Samuel, the peace which surrounded

her started a healing from the bitterness, within her heart.

The following events were to lead her into a place, where the writing of her testimony was to become the book, you are going to read.

The claustrophobia which had been with her as she entered the hall had gone and there was a ready smile on her face for all to see.

It was at three in the afternoon on a Saturday afternoon this bitter woman at the Fellowship Meeting, in the presence of God, the Creator of all, became a 'Born Again' a Christian Believing Believer, she offered herself to the true one God who calls Himself the "I Am', to do as He wished in her life.

She repented of all her past sins, and the God of Grace removed the roots of each one with one vigorous swipe, then He took the cleansed branch to be grafted into, His vine to do, His will in her life.

_**Her dedication to God, the Heavenly Father, the Creator of all, has never faltered from that day. This woman now is a Believing Believer, she believes in Jesus, and on His word, the 'Word of the Bible'**_

# PART ONE

This story is based on my faith, and written with a renewed mind, a renewed mind, which only comes through the surrendering of self, to the creator of all, our God.

I am a Believing Believer, meaning I carry with me at all times the Cross of Jesus, there is no difference to my superficial looks, the renewing is in my heart for it looks at all situations now, in the positive.

I have at all times whether asleep or awake, the lover of my soul living within me.

I have written this book, with love in my heart under the anointing of God my Heavenly Father.

This is not an entire life story, for there are parts left out as they are not at all relevant, they are the everyday happenings which we all have, and as each event unravelled there were lessons, and from these there has been time to ponder, and marvel at the awesomeness of God.

There have been many times when, I have just wanted to throw my writing away, but somehow when this happened I would be given strength to look at what was written, and see it all in a new, and brighter light again, and again.

**_Psalm 18:30, (CEV)_** your *way is perfect, Lord, and your word is correct. You are a shield for those who run to you for help.*

I learnt as I was writing to believe this scripture with all my heart. God has restored me completely; He has worked through me for His Glory and is now working through me to set captives free.

Now is the time I would like to say as Paul says in,

*2 Corinthians 4; 7 (CEV) We are like clay jars in which this treasure is stored. The real power comes from God and not from us.*

God bless each and every one of you.


## Begin with the Lord unless you want to end in failure.

This story is starting off with past and the present they jig-saw about and I must emphasize what you read is only some of my life, it is the good, the bad and the ugly times. Many have been through the same or similar situations, and there are many who will do so.

My life has and still is enjoyable; it was and is a learning process, going in circles, and mine certainly has been and still is, and as it slowly turned around, I was to experience the deep torment, of persecution, desertion, rejection and the hardest of all betrayal.

I have found though, there is always a silver lining.

And for me this happened through my introduction to yes, my creator, my God.

As my torment deepened, so did my love and commitment to Him, and Him alone.

To the one who created me, and brought me to salvation. I live in the world as a human being for this is me; I am married and have a family of four, and live a peaceful life, I know now there are two realms one natural and the other spiritual, my new life is my spiritual life, I have this promise He [God] will never leave me ever, and my husband is with me until death parts us.

I must now admit my love for, **Christ Jesus** has changed places with my husband, I look up to God first, for this is God's order, and it is my desire to be in His order of things. There are many who may say, I go on too much about this Higher Being, about His attributes, please realize though He has been so instrumental in my life, this is even before my commitment, it is part of my story, so please bear with me, and keep reading for there, is no better way to learn than through the pen of a ready writer.

God my Father, although He has total priority in my life, does not disrupt in any way my marital and family relationships; the truth is He has strengthened them.

I am going to show you there is no difficulty in bringing Christ Jesus into your home.

My home has an aura around it, not visible, but it can be felt. I have many times been asked what it is; my reply is 'Peace'.

As we go through the good, bad and ugly there maybe a situation which you will relate to. Take heart, do not falter read on, for what you are reading, these things were thrown at me, and yes I have come through them; I am now at the end of the rainbow with the pot of golden promises, Gods promises.

In life we think we can manage all our problems on our own, but somehow we run amok, well I did anyway, I would have got there, but it would have been a enormous **struggle.**

**A**s we don't live in hindsight (knowing what is in front of us, something that I am eternally grateful for) we can get hurt.

This hurt is both physical, and mental, with the mental doing the most damage, although we don't see it like that at the time.

Not only do we get hurt, we hurt others, we are selfish and very blind to this. We can get caught up in worldly situations which are almost impossible to come out of unscathed.

Basically we are all the same, for there is no one, and I mean no one, who hasn't made a mistake sometime in their lives.

We live in a human world, mistakes, offences they are both the same are part of it.

There is a tissue thin line between right and wrong, and I pray you will find as you read on, the 'Word of God' provides black and white, and removes all grey areas from Christian living.

**Spiritually, we live and write** from the heart and bypass the brain [the grey matter]

We have those who change the rules to suit their own means. This will never change; it is noticeable wherever there are stringent rules. We think we have the answers, no we don't, and it is very easy to drift off the path of rightful behaviour.

I am going to share with you, the deep torment I went through, how I coped, or didn't cope with accusations, persecution, desertion, rejection and I emphasize strongly the hardest to come to terms with was, betrayal.

And once again you will read, while I was suffering, how I was to find this 'Cross bearer' someone who gave me strength and love, a love so different from any other I have ever experienced.

It was the **Divine Love of God.**

I am going to share with you my walk towards this love, and I will share with you my life walk after I had taken Jesus into my heart.

This love is given to us quicker than the snap of the fingers.

This love – God's love, is ours for the asking if we are, prepared to come to Him on his terms. Allowing God to be in control...

We get ourselves into a pit of despair before; we utter the words which will release us from the burden, the burden hanging over us, hastily bringing about our destruction.

I was in the middle of my self-destruction, when I suddenly saw a bright shining Light, and I walked towards it. This light was the recognition of another being, a Spiritual begin, one who never forsakes us, and hasn't ever forsaken me, since my walk with Him.

As I have said I was wallowing in self-destruction, full of self-pity, when I offered a very empty and bitter heart to the Lord. But, *'Praise be'* God heard my cry.

**Psalms 40:2-3 (CEV)** *And pulled me from a lonely pit full of mud and mire. You let me stand on a rock with my feet firm, and you gave me a new song a song of praise to you.*

Without divine love and understanding in my heart, there is no way I would have been able to write this story.

I had to know positively, the creator of all. I had to be a believer and better still a **Believing Believer** I had to be filled with the Holy Spirit, the Spirit of God. I had to have the Lord at my right hand. This is explained further on so please keep reading along with me, and be encouraged, about the uncertainty of this, it does end.

Many times He has given me a gentle nudge, to rewrite a sentence when I have wandered off on some tangent of my own. I am reminded when this happens, it is with His High Authority, I am writing this.

It is with High Authority; I am writing to help anyone who feels lonely or hurt anyone who needs love and strength, anyone who feels they have been abused by society.

I praise the Lord, for all the love, He has bestowed on me, and the extra love He has given me, to spread over these pages like a balm.

When I offered myself to Him, I made a total commitment.

With this commitment I received immediately a peace which was so beautiful. This peace was given to me without hesitation.

I had been transformed quicker than any metamorphic process. Caterpillar into Butterfly.

It was instantaneous; and the beautiful thing about it was my response, it was spontaneous. My healing was then to begin.

**Philippians 4:7 (CEV)** *then, because you belong to Christ Jesus, God will bless you with peace that no one can completely understand.*

I found understanding for humbleness through my growing relationship with God. He was the only one who could make it clear, and now, years on I am able to hear Him and trust Him. Isn't this beautiful? God and I, we have a bond, it is a oneness of caring, for each other. Through my total commitment I started a new life.

*John 3:3, (CEV) Jesus replied 'I tell you for certain that you must be born from above .before you can see God's kingdom* **In verse 7,** *Don't be surprised when I say that you must be born from above'.*

I will not argue with that? I did have a lot of learning to do and the following may help you, if you are in this very situation.

Although I was filled with the Holy Spirit and believed in Jesus, I didn't always heed Him, neither a word from the Bible, or what I had in my heart. Hear this; I actually had the audacity to argue!

But the answer is very simple; I had committed my mind, but not my heart. We must, relinquish our self-will 100%.

Tough but true!

When I eventually did this my life became easier. Obeying God from then on become the most natural thing to do, for there is really no alterative unless, you want to live arguing with yourself all the time. A divided house will not stand it says, in ***Matthew 12:25*.(CEV)** Don't be misled here though, for there were many times when I was to backslide and listen to 'myself. Overcoming this comes with spiritual growth and healing, and for me this went on for four years, before I found freedom, and was able to 'Trust God'. I finally recognised **"Yes He is in control**".

Believe me I know I have not yet reached total freedom. This will only happen when I go home to my Heavenly Father.

It is the journey not the arrival, which brings understanding for this.

As a believer's spirit recognises the same in a believer, a non-believer may also recognise something, but they may not know what it is. Or deny it, for it does seem to be a little over the edge.

Many years ago I met a Born Again Christian. I wasn't when I first met her, although I saw something in her, and yes I wanted it for myself.

There was a peace about her which I could feel.

I now have this peace, and am being told there is a presence about me. I know there is, it is within me, I feel it.

Praise the Lord, for I know what I saw in her, was the special kind of peace which comes only from "JESUS".

When you get into a pit of despair, there is only one being who can get you out. For a worldly being to do so, it is not possible.

They maybe able to alleviate the problem for a short time, but at the end of the day it will still be there. I had let my problems grow into a surmountable force, of which I certainly was unable to overcome by myself.

I thought no one could help me.

How wrong I was, for I hadn't let God take complete control.

I argued I tried to put everything into categories, which was a complete waste of time, for He doesn't work that way.

*Isaiah 55:8, (CEV) 'My thoughts and my ways are not like yours'.*

There were many times when I could hear God sighing, "Here we go again". I would feel His gentle warm smile, as He waited for me to catch up, again and again. Believe me I have received many rebukes from Him; and no doubt I will receive many more.

Each time this happens I know it has been done with love for me. It is in **Revelation 3:19 (CEV) 'I correct and punish everyone I love. So make up your minds to turn away from your sins.'**

God has many names, He is the Creator, the Father in Heaven, Lord, and something I treasure, and He is my friend, a friend who takes me just as I am each day, if I am having an off day He is still there it does not put Him off, as can happen with worldly friends. They act as your judge and jury, it is to be hoped they are without sin themselves, there is an old adage with says 'people who live in glass houses should not throw stones'

What I have said, and what I am going to say, God already knows. Even the hairs on my head are counted. Although there is a finer meaning to this, basically it means God knows everything about me and you!

*Psalm 139:1 (CEV) 'You have looked deep into my heart, Lord and you know all about me'* then in verse *4 'Before I even speak a word, you know what I will say'*

I think this is really awesome. I might as well say what I am thinking, unless it will hurt someone, and then silence is, as said 'golden' I only want to love people, to never harm them. My heart is bursting as I write this, it is bursting with love, a love I can feel right down to my finger tips, it is making me want to cry, not with sadness, but with joy.

**<u>Hebrews 13:6 (CEV)</u> *'That should make you feel like saying, the Lord helps me! Why should I be afraid of what people can do to me?'***

My thinking has changed to His and His words to mine, for we need to be in unison with Him. When I started to grow spiritually I would use my Bible with hesitation, which was another reason why I argued, for I would try to analyse the word. Now I can go to my Bible with an automatic and trusting confidence. I have found there is no equal to the peace the living word can give to me. Before my day starts I like to spend time with God, praying and best of all listening out for Him. By spending this quiet time, first thing in the morning, I put myself in good stead for the day ahead. I have a choice when I wake up, to be happy, or unhappy, and I opt for the happy.

By giving thanks to God, for the day I have just had, and for looking after me while I slept, I am making the day in front of me a happy one. Being unhappy leaves the door open for alien thoughts, and feelings to come in, and make a beautiful day the absolute pits.

There are some days when my house is like a railway station, as soon as my feet hit the ground, the daily grind starts. This doesn't bother me one bit for there are no rules where you pray. I have found myself in the smallest room praying, and then I have to laugh. God does have a sense of humour never doubt it; He made me so He must know what I have to do. As long as we have peace in our hearts, we can't help but be contented.

Yesterday is history, today is a new beginning, and tomorrow will come bringing another new beginning. Do not dwell on yesterday, go forward.

All answers to our daily living are in the 'Word of God' the Holy Bible.

It is our moment by moment, hand book.

We must also learn His time isn't our time, so we must have patience.

Don't rush things, thinking our time is right, for His time is eternal, so when seeking answers learn to be patient, and learn to listen.

Having to discipline my analytical mind, was a learning process leading me to patience, I still fall short of God's Glory where patience and compassion' are concerned, but I am working on them. There were many times I would go off on some tangent of my own, but I always came up against a brick wall, there was something which would stop me. I am very thankful I was stopped, but at the time I would become pushy, thinking nothing was going to get in my way. How misguided I was. The power the Lord has for stopping us following **our** plans is something formidable.

Remember though there is also an alien side. Satan is God's, and our enemy, he will try to stop us from being in complete harmony with the Lord, our 'One True God'.

We often do blame our aches and pains on the Lord, saying, "I was stopped from doing this or that by the Lord as he didn't want me to ...." He gave me a headache etc.

Let me tell you right here and now our Father in Heaven does not hurt us, physically or mentally.

He may allow us to walk this way to show us something, but He will never hurt us with intent, Jesus is gentle.

I have no problem in testing something out, to see if it is me or the Lord, if the situation arises again, and I am given a Scripture to confirm what I've heard, I go for it.

Just take time when you are in doubt about something. If it continues don't.

Being God's chosen ones we have eternity for everything.

**As long as we listen, we will find it is really simple**. I would like you to join me in the primer class, learning to understand with your hearts, not your minds.

With our minds we only hear and understand what we want to. We must learn to hear with our ears, see with our eyes and understand with our hearts.

Understanding with our hearts will fill us with love and strength. This is what I needed at the beginning of my trauma, a trauma I am going to share with you, a trauma which lasted for several months.

We receive with God's strength a love so beautiful; this love can only come from God.

I have it in abundance, it is unconditional, unfailing never ending and as you continue, may some of this love spill over on to you.

Now we continue with the years nineteen thirties to the late nineteen nineties

### Genesis 1:27 (CEV)

*So God created humans to be like himself; he made men and women.*

I was born in a rural township, in a small country, the spring bulbs are in bloom when my birthday comes around. It seems right; somehow for me to make my entry into the world at this time. I take delight in flowers and their glorious scent.

My early life wasn't eventful, it wasn't that dull either.

As in everyone's life there is a lot of learning, some of this is enjoyable, and some of it isn't. Either way the learning process is always on going for me, as I am basically a nosy person.

There were many details I put on my inbuilt computer, details needed for living in this world of pain, and sin.

I learnt the fine art of good manners, and with this we have etiquette, for finesse.

I learnt to discipline my mouth when I was young, something I believe to be very important, (a discipline we all need). I learnt to keep a quiet counsel, **for he who repeats a confidence is a fool.**

I learnt how to differentiate between the nonsensical, the serious and the fads of the time.

My youth wasn't any different to the children in the nineteen, nineties.

When I was born a world war had just started. I am sure there is no significance there. I myself have no memory of the war, what I know about it has been learnt since. I do not like war, or fighting of any sort.

To me, they are a waste of time and certainly a waste of precious lives. Although they do happen, and are still happening, as I see it they are usually from someone's greed or religion and the need of power, there are so many topics which could be written in here as reasons; I will desist from doing so.

I have tried to remember something from my birth to my starting school, the memories I get are so faint I am unable to say if they are reality or something I wish had happened.

We come to my schooling now.

I went to a small country school about eight kilometres; it was miles then away from where I lived as a child.

I have no idea how I went to school, but I do have recollections of walking home, for I remember once, eating some dates the village grocer had given me to take home.

A telling off a on my arrival would have been administered, for I am sure I would have eaten most of them, I was told I had whether true or not, this I do not know.

I never liked school in fact it has a distinct memory of hurt, for I am a plain girl and I found it very hard to make friends. Being quiet and excessively shy is a put off.

My secondary education was at the nearest township, at the local High School, it has changed its name now, as places of education go with the times. I do have a memory of going in a bus which looked like a square tin on wheels, and of course it was called the 'biscuit tin'.

I don't believe there were any signs of genius in me, I would call myself average.

Looking back I didn't liked secondary school either, in fact as I deliberate over it, to me schooling was the pits.

The one thing I did excel at was running. I was really good; I would represent my school in the county school competitions. This didn't teach me how to read and write, something I have mastered as you can see. I didn't learn to be competitive either. I have abhorrence for competition, although in life while growing up, we are encouraged to win all the time.

In hindsight, I have learnt more since leaving school, as experience teaches, but I am very grateful for my basic training at school.

I do not want to give you the impression schooling is unnecessary, just scrub the idea, it is very important for our future, although when we are young it doesn't enter minds there is a reason for it.

Without the three R's reading, riting, rithmetic we can create problems, which cause difficulties as we grow older. I have had first hand experience with those who have been unable to read and write.

I tutored adult students in this area, and I know each one of those students will endorse schooling is important.


Be thankful if you are able to have an education, and take the opportunity with both hands.

We have come now to another learning episode in my life; one I shared with my sister, four and a half years my junior.

Yes she was born after the war!

My sister and I would ride our bikes along unsealed country roads to Sunday school.

There were very few children from our village area who didn't go; it was the accepted thing to do. The roads we rode on were very rough, and it was a challenge going there, for if we rode into potholes which were deep we could fall off our bikes, this happened most times. Woe to the pretty clothes.

I enjoyed the Bible stories; I liked the teacher, for she was a lovely kind old lady who wore a grey pin striped suit, to me this seems to be relevant, the one with the long jacket. I have always wanted one.

Now-a-days there are many of us who are unable to afford to buy a new one like it, and will search out the second hand clothing shops for the very same jacket style.

This style has come back year after year.

Thinking about my Sunday school teacher, I doubt very much if she would have been very old.

Age when I was young seemed to be in two categories, young like Mum and Dad, or old like my grandparents.

There were no in betweens.

As our teacher was unmarried, well she had to be old didn't she? Why you say, I don't know it was through the eyes of a child.

Once a month we would go to the family church service.

This was a novelty. There was no Sunday school, which meant no bike ride; we could go in the car.

I vividly remember the car it was my Grandfather's. It was a big square heavy looking car. When we went for a drive it seemed to take forever to get there, sixty miles as it was then, might as well have been six hundred.

The trips seemed to take longer than the time we spent visiting.

In actual fact it wasn't that bad, and everyone always enjoyed themselves.

Just a child's impression, the same with the car, it looked so big. It was an Armstrong Siddley, a late 1920's model.

If I saw it now I would probably wonder why I had thought it was so big.

This tuition, in Sunday school and church was to lay a foundation stone for the life I now lead, but if someone told me it would help in my future I certainly would never have understood.

I taught Sunday school for a while, I am unable to remember very much about it, but I am certain of one thing I would never have voluntarily offered my services, my Mother will have done it for me, as I have already mentioned I suffered from acute shyness. I followed the family trend though, and sang in the local choir, as did my Mother and paternal Grandfather. I was brought up in the era when it was 'to be seen and not heard'; well that was the idea.

There was no free speech for minors in my youth! If I tried, I would receive a look which would freeze a river over, or a stinging slap. I do remember trying to put my two bit in, it didn't work. My sister and I were brought up in a Christian household, doing what was expected of us, we lived the day peacefully and at bedtime said out prayers 'gentle Jesus meek and mild. Our habit prayer for neither of us would have had any true understanding if it. The reason being it was never explained to us, just as going to Church and Sunday school, they were what one did on Sundays.

I was the Girl Guide, my sister was taught the piano.

What I learnt at Guides I put on my inbuilt computer, and these things contributed to the writing of my first knitting book.


This next learning experience is just something else.

It was the dancing lessons; they were out of orbit, to borrow a phrase. Once a week through the winter months, a very brave lady, came to the village hall, to teach the girls how to dance. After school the girls would trudge over to community hall, in the local domain.

You would always find these halls in the 'old days'. They were an icon to a district and always in use by the community.

We, the girls put ourselves into this teacher's hand, to see if she could instil some rhythm into us. I am still able to remember the steps, toe, heel, shuffle toe heel. My rhythmic attributes seemed to be non existent. This was fortunate; I hadn't wanted to be a dancer.

So endeth my dancing career. We put on a concert once, where we showed off our adeptness in dancing. Also I suppose it was to show the parents the fees being paid hadn't been wasted. One was never to know there might be a promising dancer in our midst.

I don't recall this actually happening.

As I have mentioned, I can still remember the dance steps, but if I try to do them now there is neither elegance nor fitness evident.

I did and still have, an avid love for classical music; I always have it playing near me as I write. I have classical music, playing on one radio and at the same time the Christian radio station, on another.

The Living words of the Bible flow beautifully with classical music.

This gives me a peace when writing, unless I become conscious the classical has become too sonorous and reverberating then I have to physically turn it off. This happened to me one day when typing, and the lesson from it stays vividly with me to never underestimate the hand of God.

I have gone from past to present here, no doubt I will do it many times again, but it doesn't really matter, for I am writing in the present about the past.

The silence after I switched the rather too loud classical music off was very significant, and as I was trying to collect my thoughts again, reading what I had written, there seemed to be something amiss, I just couldn't see what it was, but I knew I had been disturbed for some reason. I read back through earlier typed paragraphs, everything made sense to me.

The Christian radio station which was still playing quietly in the background, suddenly it became louder, and I mean louder.

I know I never touched the switch; never mind suddenly the announcer had my full attention. I started to laugh, for he quoted what I had just written, also telling his listeners where the Bible reading was, I looked it up and yes my version was incorrect and could be, misleading. Praise the Lord, for we are told emphatically in the book of Revelations not to add or take away prophetic words from the Bible.

I praised the Lord for the interruption with my work, and the chance to change the two incorrect words.

The Lord, has said anyone who removes or adds something to the prophetic words will be punished, and I know I was being warned. We must never forget the words from the Bible must hold the same truth whatever the situation. *'As on earth as in Heaven'*

## *Revelations 22:18, 19. (CEV)*

I must share this with you while the announcer was reading; I turned around to see if he was reading over my shoulder. The man up there can bring hilarity into our lives.

I receive the same peace when near the sea as from the Bible and from music.

The words of encouragement I get from this beautiful book are like a lullaby, there is stillness, tranquillity, and only living with the Lord are we able to go into the past again without pain and strife.

I was brought up on a farm in a secure environment. It was and is a beautiful way to live. Life then was so simple. The relaxed atmosphere we had doesn't seem to be so apparent now. Like many lifestyles, they have become a businesslike. To really enjoy them, you need plenty of money in the bank or you have it as a hobby.

I have lived and breathed farming all my life, and the man I married was a farmer, it is the only lifestyle I really know, it is in my blood.

Anyone who lives on a farm of small to average scale, who has a modest bank balance, will know what it is like making ends meet.

We sell the wool and the grain from our crops, a cheque comes in, and it helps tidy up loose ends, but the overflow if there is any has to go back into the farm. This is if we want crops next year.

It is a vicious cycle, and sometimes it can be almost cruel. As I have said I know what I am speaking about having been there. Times can be very tough almost unfair.

**Ecclesiastes** says it all. *There is a time for everything. Why chase the wind? It has all happened before.*

Our living was frugal; we learnt how to live within our means so there would be plenty to go around. **'Give us today the food we need,'** pretty simple isn't it. The Lord's Prayer mentions our daily bread; remember here though man cannot live on bread alone, we need God's Word as well.

To an unbeliever, it is too simple to believe; I understand this, so whatever your farm is like, believer or unbeliever go for it, farming either way is a great way to live. I have seen and been guilty myself, of farming the neighbours farm, it is easier, as well as bringing up his children, the learning here is the critical finger should be the helping hand. We must love our neighbours.

**Neighbour,** doesn't necessarily mean the people who live beside us, it has a wider definition, someone or something which is near another.

Modern technology has brought along bigger machinery, also with this there are new and bigger problems. But the balance is there.

Basically farming has the same chores whatever the era.

After I had left my schooling behind me I went to work at a guesthouse which wasn't very far from my home.

I did enjoy this, but found my shyness wasn't an asset. Through my experience of shyness, I did my best to make sure my own children were not smitten with it.

It was almost an illness with me. Sometimes I feel as if I have never actually out grown this malaise, for I am still happy in my own company.

I have now the choice to be with people or not.

There is something as a 'spirit filled' Christian, to be alone doesn't matter, for we are never on our own, are we?

I am not oblivious to the fact I need fellowship. Also I wouldn't be doing the work which was ordained for me by God, if I stay put in my own four walls.

I have an obligation to spread the Good Word with joy to all people. I can grieve the Holy Spirit or fellowship with God. It seems easier and more beneficial to go for the latter.

My parents were kindness itself, both of them would be available if help was ever needed in the district, I remember there were very few times when we didn't have a relative living with us, a relative who needed care.

I have mentioned there was very little money for my husband and me; it was harder for my parents. My sister and I always had lovely clothes; our Mother would sew for us all hours of the night. Times were tough; you have to be living in a similar situation to appreciate just how tough it may have been for them both. I can now see how tough.

We always had plenty to eat, even if there was homemade butter. I loathed the smell, the taste, everything about it. I also disliked my Grandfather's Emulsion.

He always had it; it is strange how I still can remember it, because he died when I was ten, we were offered it, and to be sure it was an offer only taken up on once. I can even smell it while I am typing!

I didn't like Horlicks either.

Being of a skinny build when I was younger, it was thought I needed nourishment.

This was a sentiment I never shared with my parents.

As children of the 1940's and 1950's we were never expected to do other than accept things without question. I don't believe this rule did us any harm.

Life seems to have become competitive now, it most probably was back then as well, but certainly not noticeable to anyone who was young, it seems we are involved with status symbols now, where there is very little individuality, we have become an 'en masse' nation. Maybe it is a phase to out grow.

Nations seem to have become very greedy for power. We only need to read the headline news.

In the end time there are going to be losers. The way to find our real worth is to find Jesus. I believe we all need to have someone, to hold on to so we can live in a balanced world. We must learn to recognise there is a spiritual world even if it is unseen.

Living with God is the positive way to live, and this is a way we can learn to use our faith. We have all been given a measure of faith, how we activate it is entirely our choice. What we believe is our choice.

It is not for me to make it for you.

Someone who had tremendous faith was my Dad. He was a beautiful man, although at times like anyone, he sometimes became misguided.

I think the contributing factor to his faith was his upbringing.

His Mother died when he was only a few months old.

She was expecting her fifth child, and typhoid fever took them both, Dad was her fourth child.

I have always found this very sad somehow. I wish I had known her; I may well have done so in Dad, for he also had the same open countenance evident on her face in the photos I have seen.

Mother, my sister and I had a time of grieving as Dad passed over. His illness was for such a short time, and was all over in six weeks so he didn't suffer for too long. Something I am very grateful for.

I felt a great loss when he died; he was in his early sixties, very young.

It is very strange for while I am writing this final copy, I have learnt one of my parent's best friends has succumbed to cancer which has made it possible for me to bid her farewell, which I now do.

I had great admiration for this lovely gentle lady.

Although I am unable to see my Dad, I no longer have any questions as to why he died so young. It is not for us to question the ways of the Lord.

These feelings have gone as time is the healing factor.

I am now able to remember him without the sadness death can bring. I have joy in remembering his life, and celebrate it with a thankful heart for what I learnt from him, these things have contributed to the person I am now.

There is no doubt in my mind we need someone to believe in and no time is better than when a loved one is taken from us. He had his time and I know he served God's purpose on earth. Wherever you are Dad I love you, and I will always remember the good times we had, with love in my heart.


## *Matthew 19; 6*

### *Therefore, what God has joined together let not man separate.*

The generation I was brought up in believed, once you married you stayed at home to look after your husband and children. This was the pattern for my married life and I accepted it as the rule. I still do.

I married, in the early sixties; a man who was a year older than me. We were married in the church where I went wearing my very best clothes to the family church services.

In summer it was the Panama hat, with white lacy gloves, in winter, warm coats, berets and knitted gloves.

My sister and I heard, constantly on the way home to change our clothes straight away or else! Who is afraid of the big bad wolf? I use to mutter under my breath. I changed my clothes though.

Church goers today dress causally, great changes from my youth; we seemed to be prim and proper. Clothes don't maketh the man. Huh?

As for my wedding, I changed the Panama hat for a veil and tiara, and my gown was cream brocade.

As white represents purity, my choice of cream gave for speculation. Never mind if you ever see me in white chalk it up, for having an olive complexion it doesn't look too good on me, it was said once I looked 'like death warmed up'.

It was also said as I chose a colour I must be pregnant. How great is the supposition of people. My husband and I had difficulty remembering our wedding service, but we did have a precious document telling us it took place, forty four years ago, this number will change, but the date of the marriage won't.

For the first three years, we were on our own; this gave us the chance to become really good friends, as well as husband and wife.

We were able to learn each other's idiosyncrasies, and there were plenty of them, in fact as we grew older, we seem to develop more.

Backing up again, when I was fifteen, I developed a blood disorder.

This would hospitalise me for many weeks at a time, and was a continual occurrence over the years.

It was just a matter of learning again.

I learnt to live within my limitations, which made things easier maybe not for those in the family but it did for me. My treatment was anticoagulation's, to dissolve the clots, or if you prefer thrombosis, which often travelled to my lungs.

I did not enjoy this way of living, for there were so many things I wanted to do, and if I set out to do them, something would go wrong and I would end up in hospital, it seem to go with the complaint, and there was very little I could do about it.

My illness wasn't compatible with carrying a baby full term, and I had several miscarriages. The family members will say this is an understatement. They are correct, but I have no wish to dwell on what wasn't. There was a natural sadness at the time, but if I hadn't had them, the next part of my story may not have been.

In the middle sixties, we adopted a little girl, our first little October girl.

When we brought her home as our daughter, she was only a few days old.

Our excitement on the way to the hospital to get her was almost as great as our nervousness. We had a little pram, and I had collected a trousseau for her, I knitted and knitted from the moment our name went on the adoption system list. I had little jackets already knitted, but I wanted to have new things for our special little baby.

Not knowing if we would be given a boy or a girl had made the waiting exciting. We could have said which gender we wanted but it never entered our heads to do so. When we the call came through to ask if we wanted a little girl I was so happy, and as I was home on my own at the time I couldn't say yes please, I had to wait until my husband came home to ask him, and of course he said yes.

On the tenth day off we went to pick up our little girl. I had taken in a gown; a jacket, vest, nappies and a shawl, all collected with love, to bring our little baby girl home. I remember when I was dressing her, at the hospital I was all thumbs, and the nurse had to help me.

Our first glimpse of her was 'oh so beautiful' she was asleep, we could hardly contain ourselves wanting to get away to have a really good look at her.

We had this chance on the way home, for we pulled off to the side of the road, and had our special moment together.

Two had become three.

When I mention the fact Mothers, who carry a baby to birth are automatically being prepared for the work ahead, not everyone agrees with me, but I still believe there has been a preparation going on.

I didn't have this with our first little girl, although I didn't give birth to her, my body did respond to the situation.

Having carried a baby for a short time before a miscarriage, or maybe we just wanted a baby, was the reason.

After the first day with a baby in the house, I felt we had become over zealous.

Maybe we weren't meant to have babies. It stays vividly in my mind the first morning I bathed her, feed her, and then put her back in her little bassinet thinking, wow I have finished. Then I remembered there was washing to be done.

There were no disposables in my day. With the washing on the line, now time, for a lovely cup of tea.

Oh, no, the man likes to eat, and he would be in soon for his lunch.

We had a meal, then, wham, bam, baby time again.

What had I been doing before we were blessed with this dear little girl, she was absolutely delightful?

When she was one, we had naturally this time another little girl; she arrived in October, medical science had developed a new drug, and I was able to carry a baby full term.

We now had two little girls, both with dark hair, dark eyes, and both very beautiful.

Three had become four.

The baby boom continued in our family with a little boy, born two years later, then another little boy, born the following year. We now had two of each. Four became five, and five became six.

I was seriously ill after our last little boy was born. My blood complaint really complained.

He was five months old when eventually I was able to go home from hospital to stay.

I did go out on two occasions; neither time being successful; had I become too reliant on the hospital care, was the question running through my head?

I did get home though, with my health becoming a serious problem.

On my tenth wedding anniversary as a gift, (ha) once again through medical science, I had a major operation, which was to change my life for the better.

The operation was to have a Vena Cava plication, inserted into my Vena Cava artery, and at the same time I had a hysterectomy.

The Vena Cava sieve to stop big clots going to my lungs, and the hysterectomy speaks for itself. Anyway both of these operations have been a success.

Before our first little girl was born, we had bought a farm, so the children started their childhood on a farm like I did.

As all farmers' wives know, they are very often asked to become the unpaid help. I never minded, this was the life we had chosen, so naturally I did help, expecting the same help from him, and yes receiving it sometimes!

There were times when it did become frustrating though, this would be when I was busy with the baking, or some other chore of equal importance to **ME**, when there was a call out. I would go, but I must admit I would be muttering under my breath about the unfairness of being the housekeeper, as well as the farm worker.

Many of you will have been there not necessarily on a farm but you will have been asked to do something, at sometime or other.

The children went to the same country school I went to, they went to the same Sunday school, also the family church service, which was still once a month.

One girl learnt to play the piano, the other was the Brownie. While they were learning the piano, and the Brownie rules, the little boys were learning the basics of farming.

The learning process had started again; this is a process which will go on for the rest of their lives.

Being a Mother, you become a nurse, teacher, doctor, a vet for the children's pets; a mechanic for the toys and bikes, the list goes on and on. The amazing thing is I was able to achieve all of these accomplishments without any diplomas. Now who said I wasn't a genius?

A very important achievement I mastered was the art of diplomacy. I became a good listener; I was able to listen to the children's 'anthills', a name I gave their problems. I was able to listen without comment and when they had finished their tirade I would give them a hug and say, 'that is a bit of a worry,' they would then laugh, and go off to play.

My reaction was really what they were looking for; when there wasn't one it was 'all is well'. They were being guided. There is nothing like a kindly ear, and we all need one at times. Their serious 'anthills' were dealt with accordingly.

It is a tremendous responsibility, being a Mother. We are the centre figure in a little universe, which is our home and family.

When we ourselves are happy, they will be happy; when we are irritable they will be irritable. I often felt like screaming, did sometimes, but soon scrubbed the idea.

It created a small volcano, each one wanted to have a go, and to make it worse, they did it at the same time.

Following example is another way of learning. Parents do lead the way for their children's future.

I wasn't very good at self-control; for a while anyway. After a few upsets, major ones, I soon got the idea to cool down girl, or start a war.

I learnt when to go outside, and kick the woodshed door. This is one of those family jokes which stick, like many jokes about 'Mother', they are remembered.

When our woodshed door collapsed with weather rot, the children's father, and I thanked him very much for it, told the elder son I was the culprit and had kicked it in.

Whenever anything went wrong after that, to be sure, it was said 'Mum will kick the woodshed door in'

There are such a lot of little things in families which are great to hold on to, and we, "Mother's" can use them later on when we have grandchildren. Ha! Ha! Dream on! Times change and our jokes are called, 'sick mum'

My second daughter and I had our own message for one another if through the day, if there was occasion when I had to pull rank on her, I would put a little pink plastic pig, in her bed at night.

This little act, would be reversed if she felt I had encroached upon her privacy through the day. Yes, the little pig would be in my bed.

We used a plastic pig to say 'I love you"

We took the children with us when we went for a holiday; we didn't have many, though for I wasn't a very brave Mother, and I didn't have the diploma in the 'holiday management technique'. Six going on a holiday was quite a feat to conquer.

Families wherever they are, or whoever they are mean work.

One time we went off in the caravan on our own, when I took out the sugar basin, the little pig was there, I wanted to go home straight away, but stayed the course, giving the hug on my return.

Every moment is precious when you have a family, and with me going into hospital so many times they were more so. We knew our children would one day grow up, and go their own ways; didn't we ourselves do this?

The bond of love with our children is so special, it is a bond which can be very fragile and doesn't always stay, children become adults and as individuals they have their own lives to live and parents can get in the way. This isn't meant to happen, but it can.

We treated our gifts from God, with the love they had been given to us; for this is what children are gifts from God.

Do not be mistaken in thinking, the years we were bringing our family up didn't bring along problems, sometimes hardship.

We weren't flushed with money, as I have said; we like my parents through choice, had an almost frugal existence, we had everything we needed though and we mustn't forget, there were six of us to feed and clothe.

Each time a problem came along; we were able to overcome it, and in doing so the children, learnt to be strong and supportive of each another.

There have been times, when I borrowed a few cents from a child to buy the milk, for when the milkman came down the road, there would be the mad rush to put the bottles out, worse still there would be a madder rush to find the money. And before you pick me up on that comment, we didn't have a milking cow

The children didn't begrudge giving it to me, we may have heard about it every time we used the milk, but the few cents which were precious, had been given readily. This is family support.

When you have four children as close as ours, their shoes would all go at the same time, but it was worst first, and the children accepted this.

We can be very thankful for we never encouraged our decisions to be treated any other way, than with acceptance. There were squabbles, no family gets away without them. It all comes down to learning again.

Respect has to be earned and they did their best to learn this. As parents we coped with the task, guiding the children along the path of good living and beliefs. It was hard work at times, but we certainly did our best. Each day we had something to be thankful for.

Our little family truly blessed us.

Life is full of learning and another lesson was drawing closer for me, one as a Mother I found very hard. It was the letting go of the children as they felt the need to spread their wings, and leave home.

I have nothing against anyone else's children leaving home, but when it is your own, it is very different.

They have their rights though the same as we did. We must let go if we want them to develop into adults achieving for themselves, the goals they want to reach in their own lives. It is important we allow this, and it is a test for us in trusting them, let go, but always be there to give your support if it is needed.

Now all the lessons about diplomacy, and quiet counsel were put into practice. I am very thankful I actually passed the test. Managing to leave things unsaid not to interfere, well not too much anyway!

It is easy to bring up someone else's children, as I have commented, 'if it were me, I would have.' I had to bite my tongue many times, but as I have commented, I did bite my tongue and leave the words unspoken.

Eventually the time came when the numbers around the table began to dwindle.

As parents we made a few ground rules, which I believe a parent has the right to do. Whichever way you look at it we made the rules, and one by one off they went.

In our home, rules meant love and, security. This is the game you play with caution, play it right and they will always come home.

I must say, it will be when it suits them, but they will come. Play it wrong and you may very well lose them. It takes a long time for children to get to where we are in life, and there are times when they may never understand what we did was really a guideline for them.

Old heads do not fit young shoulders!

Some families only see each other at weddings or funerals; the sad thing is they may only live a few kilometres apart. Notice kilometres, instead of miles. I'm getting the hang of it.

We have been lucky, we played the game right, and our children come back as they please; they all know an invitation is not necessary to return to the home nest.

This nest is wherever we are living; things the children grew up with are theirs as well.

I must say they have depleted over the years for they themselves have taken their favourite items. I had no argument with this. My Mother did the same; she was only too pleased for my sister and me to have some family treasures.

They are only treasured as family history. (Just Sentimental Value). Not treasures stored in heaven.

One day while I was out, our second daughter came in and raided the cake tins. She left a note saying thanks and apologised for the crumbs left on the bench. Over a span of a few weeks her memory had weakened, she was unable to remember were the dishcloth was kept. Hadn't forgotten where the cake tins were though!

I loved it when they came in, and they did this as often as they were able to, and each one knew they had the freedom to do so, it is from the stem of love.

Remember here they are still growing up into the adult world, and it does not always treat you kindly.

The boys would come in and make themselves, a block of cheese sandwich. The girls well one lived further away, but I know if she had visited there would have been sheets of music everywhere. Each child had his or her own trade mark.

One girl tied a teddy bear by the neck on a door handle once; I removed the poor thing asking her later on why she had done it? There was no reason, and as I was walking away I heard her say 'How did Mum know it was me?' I ask you? Mothers are very well tuned in with their offspring.

Our family are all living their own lives now, things have changed this was inevitable, both our boys have never forgotten their parentage and I am pleased they know they are welcome home anytime along with their own families, even though their home has change its locality. There were no ties made by us, for emotional blackmail can be a deterrent for anybody. It is out there just not recognised. We must not demand.

## *Colossian 3:21*

**Parents do not irritate your children, or they will become discouraged. Hallelujah.**

It wasn't until the children left home I realised what silence was. I was amazed at it. I had never realised how much noise there is in a family home. The chatter, music, laughter, crying, yes the silence…

At long last my hubby and I could play the music we liked and actually hear it without some loud band blaring from a child's room drowning it out. The times I was told 'not to be old fashion' or 'you are hearing the latest' as if it was a great honour. There was one comment which received a snort 'when you were young'. I have to laugh as I am writing this, for these comments have been said before; I know I said them to my parents, and I know my folk did not like listening to Beethoven at full volume.

We have just about completed a full circle, for the four children have families of their own now. I am a grandmother; I have joined the 'Granny' syndrome. When my sister and I had a different opinion to our Mother she use to say, 'my day is coming, I am going to sit back and watch you with your children"

My girls argued with me. Mostly about clothes, but they did argued, and always staged their performance in front of their Grandmother, to get reinforcement I suppose, when this happened I would see the smile upon her face which said, 'been there done that'.

The family which started with two, then grew to six, has started the next generation and these numbers have increase over the years. We are not together very often as a complete family, but whenever we are we have a lot of fun. It is great to see how rules change, we are in another decade, one where we are still learning, and we watched our children being put through their paces by their children.

I use to hear my Mother saying when sis and I were in our teens, her education had just started. I now know there is a ring of truth in it.

Our second daughter and her family live in Australia she is a working Mother, and has achieved for herself the merit of being a fully qualified nurse.

The other daughter is also a working Mother.

To get to either flying it takes three hours In both cases it might as well be three years. I have said many times I would like to talk to one of my girls, I wished they lived closer, they have chosen their own lives, and I pray they are happy with their choice.

If your daughters live near you, be eternally thankful. I would love to see mine every day, well maybe every second day, well maybe once in a while, either way it would be lovely to have them nearby.

We were thanked for taking them to see things, with special mention about the seals on one of our holidays. Those seals must have made an impression, for when she came home once; it was one of the things she wanted to show her daughter. Somehow this made everything as parents, seem well worth the experience.

As all Mothers know, as the day ends, the last meal over the children in their beds, the tidying up all finished, it is a very good feeling to either sit down, or fall into bed, ourselves.

### *Romans 8:28 CEV*

*We know that God is always at work for the good of everyone who loves him.*

The learning has never stopped, and I now entered into another phase, with me still in the home.

With all the children away fitting into their own niche I had to master the art of cooking for two, not the army, I had to stop filling the saucepan with potatoes, I had to learn how to make a small apple pie and who wants to eat chocolate cake for weeks, trying to beat the mould. After many attempts with a few ingredients wasted as well as my time I eventually got there. As I peeled two potatoes, I would think 'this isn't enough' then peel two more, and when my hubby came in he would ask, 'who was coming for dinner?' Don't you love him? The times I did this, I wonder now if I was subconsciously hoping the children would walk in. This did happen.

The times when I managed to get it right, only enough for two!

Who hasn't been there one-way or other?

By this time we were no longer farming. We had moved house and began working for a government department.

Farming was out the door and the topic of discussion, became water, yes water everywhere. This was a totally new life style along with new phraseology, after farming this life seemed to be restful, although as we both found out there were rush times. One and the most important were in the peak of an irrigation season, in mid summer, when everyone wants water.

We stayed in this lifestyle for thirteen years, although, farming did draw my farmer man, and he bought a little land, where he was able to run a few sheep. Once a farmer always a farmer it has been said.

In the late eighties he was diagnosed as being a diabetic.

Once again we were off on a learning spree, although it was him with the complaint, it certainly involved us both. A year before this diagnosis, the quiet good-natured man whom I had married changed.

It was like living with a time bomb.

It didn't take very much for him to explode, the least little thing going wrong and he would become a stranger, his tolerance fuse was very short.

Living like this did put a strain on our lives. There were many occasions when I didn't know whether to speak or not, just in case I had my head bitten off. This led to ghastly silences.

These were very noticeable, you could feel the tension, and even the children would ask what was wrong with Dad, before and after they had received a sharp retort.

This became once again a woodshed 'kick in' not the door this time, the whole shed. And it became apparent something was drastically amiss when we went to stay with our elder girl for the birth, of her first baby he was so ill. I always seemed to be in tears, it was the emotional side causing me to react. Diabetes has become very common, it seems to be more so now in this era, especially with older people.

It isn't at all pleasant for the person who has it, as well as the family who live with it.

This is made easier for all when medical treatment is prescribed; and as there are more than one type of diabetes it is very wise to go to a medical advisor.

With married couples there are many changes, as certainly did with us. I am not going to put them into categories, for everyone is different.

I married my hubby because I loved him.

In my marriage vows I said 'in sickness and in health'.

Please notice sickness comes first, the act of making love is a very minor part of a loving relationship.

I never wanted anything other than for him, to get well, so I was prepared to go through the difficult times with him until he was stabilized with his medication.

I remember the times when I was ill, the many times he was called to the hospital, for the outcome of my illness was unpredictable. He had at those times twenty fold more stress than I ever had with his diabetes. The beautiful man I married who was such fun to live with was back again, he was having his injections, his diet watched by the cook 'me' and his sugar count checked by the blood tests he did himself.

With all of this we once again come back to a peaceful path of life.

There was readjusting my cooking again. He was on a sugar free diet so I began cooking with a sugar substitute.

At the beginning, of this new phase I would cook two meals, for some reason I had the idea what he ate was not for me. The way I behaved one would think it was poison.

I soon scrubbed my way of thinking and started to eat the same.

Guess what, I didn't have any ill effects.

There was the sweet issue. Puddings!

He liked them and I was not that fussed. He had his puddings

I found so many recipes for diabetic puddings, and all were tasty.

Eventually we both were enjoying the food I cooked. I found there was very little difference, and enjoyed both the cooking as well as eating food cooked with a sugar substitute.

I have found I was feeling healthier for it too, and have continued this way ever since; sugar is not for me, maybe not for you either. I have learnt to discipline my self-indulgences.

Sometimes!! These are the quiet sneak of chocolate. We are not going to write about them though.

We are now coming to another time in my life for me to be strong, for my Mother, my family, and my sister's family.

In the middle eighties, my sister developed a terminal illness, this resulted in her having several operations, with each one taking their toll upon her.

Throughout her illness this little sister of mine was so courageous.

I have marvelled at how cancer patients become so strong mentally as their time draws closer for them to depart this earth. I know they must receive God's strength. Some may know where their strength comes from, as equally there will be those who don't.

God stays with them giving them sufficient strength to help in the time of departure.

One day while I was with her, and as she was sleeping I felt tears falling down my face, suddenly she opened her eyes. "What are you crying for?" There was absolute disgust in her voice. That was my little sister straight to the point.

We had lived together for so many years with our parents, and shared our first married years living close to each other; it was at this time though we were closer than we had ever been. We talked about the times I had been ill; shouldn't it be me to die first? For was I not the elder? We were brought up to think this way; the elder child is the first one to be married, so why shouldn't the elder child die first?

This is not God's plan at all, this is in the head of man, and man's plans do run amok!

She was a blue eyed, blonde and pretty, also very sociable, the complete opposite to me, I am dark haired olive skinned with brown eyes. It was at this time we talked about things we had never mentioned to each other before.

Emotional times, call for nothing but the truth.

She told me she had always envied me; this is so stupid, for I am just me.

The smile she gave me and the hug, for she put her thin arms around my neck, as well as the things she told me, I will remember for the rest of my life.

She gave me strength, and her love for my future. A future, without my little sister.

Her last weeks were spent in her home, with our Mother nursing her. She just wanted to be near the precious hills of our family home.

The hills we had grown up with, seeing every day, we knew this would make her final curtain call a little happier.

Also she was with her three sons, preparing them for the inevitable.

### *John 14: 1 to 18 CEV*

This was the little verse I read at her funeral. The same one I read at our Dads.

She passed away in the late eighties. Once again there was a time of grieving. There was a loss of a wife, the loss of a daughter for our Mother, I lost my little sister, her three boy's loss was harder, for they lost their Mother, and there was the loss of a beloved Auntie, for my children and for my hubby a sister-in-law.

Through this time of grieving we helped one another. It wasn't without incident, but eventually most of the problems were overcome.

Patience and time can heal wounds. And leave us with beautiful memories.

Mother and I were left now; the family which was four had become smaller.

There were many times when I was so lonely without my little sister and my Dad, and it took time as expected to overcome this, it has been done now leaving me with memories of the good fun times. It is strange the first three letters of funeral are 'FUN'

She was like our Dad, I am meant to be like my Mum, I can see several similarities between us, but they are all mannerisms., Mum and I were practical women, farm living made us this way. I have a creative nature all from my head; Mother created, the difference was her creativity all came from a pattern this does not decry it though; everything her hands made was outstandingly beautiful. Little Sis has a business mind.

My creativity could create small disasters for as a writer my ideas did not wait for the slake time they came when they came. My mother would never leave a meal cooking to go off, and do some typing, I would and did this many times, what should have been two sentences typed would turn into a lot of typing. I would forget what I was meant to be doing, and become immersed with my story, and then the ghastly smell of something burnt would hover around.

The times I have burnt a dinner is uncountable, I was only going to type the sentence I thought of while preparing the meal.

This doesn't make me sloppy, I am far from it, and the cleaning of a burnt pan soon makes one disciplined in this area.

With Christian growth I have learnt self-discipline has me having a typing schedule. There is a time for everything.

We can read about that in ***Ecclesiastes 3. CEV***

I believe we need to be true to ourselves and not too worried, and we won't take that any further, just be ourselves and do our own thing. I know I look like my mother, for I have been told so many times I accept it, but it still does not make me, her. I am totally me, let's say as my hubby often said to me 'you are a one off Charlie' and it freed me somehow.

***Proverbs 15:31 CEV***

***Healthy correction is good, and if you accept it, you will be wise***

From this wisdom I was able to go further and have mother's and my souls tie broken off me. This was a tie which I didn't realise I had, and it was this tie which made me wary of my mother always, she sometime scared me, I felt as if I was suffocating, I had to be myself to grow with God, and my very own personality is me.

This was my time for a shake up. There are many burdens we carry and never know it until we give ourselves to a Higher Power.

This may sound scary, do not worry about it if you do not understand, it is not a problem.

Our lives are about timing, and at the right time there will be understanding for you.

I was to receive a scripture, which was a comfort to my weary soul.

***Hebrew 12:2 CEV***

***We must keep our eyes on Jesus, who leads us and makes our faith complete.***

# PART TWO

We have at last travelled fifty one years.

I feel rather apologetic for this is a very condensed version of the beginning of my life. It may not read very exciting for the most it borders on the mundane, I have enjoyed it though, the good times are remembered, and the bad times are forgotten

If a lesson had to be learnt from either the good or the bad it has been put it on my inbuilt computer, marked as experience.

I lived each day as it came, there was little else I could do, and on reflection there is really no part I would like to relive.

I could say to bring the children up again, knowing what I know now. In hindsight it could have helped some situations, but they have all grown up with compassion for the elderly, and the sick, as well as the downtrodden. They have learnt to know one another; and to me that is very important.

Parental support was always there for them, still is if they need it. They can be assured we will always be there for them while we are on this earth.

*Psalm 128: 2-3CEV*

*Your fields will produce, and you will be happy and all will go well. Your wife will be as fruitful as a grapevine, and just as an olive tree is rich with olives.* There you have the confirmation, for what I have written about a Mother being the centre of a little universe the home and the family.

Isn't that beautiful?

When I first wrote about Mothers I hadn't found that confirmation. Praise the Lord!

What a beautiful book the Bible is. What a beautiful guide it is for us. It is the best guideline we can have. All or nothing, how about that?


*__Proverbs 3:5 CEV__*

***With all your heart you must trust the Lord and not your own judgement.***

*__1 Peter 2:23 CEV__*

***Although he was abused, he never tried to get even. When he suffered, he made no threats. Instead, he had faith in God who judges fairly.***

The daily running of my life changed in the early nineties.

This change was dramatic, and traumatic, it was so out of proportion with the before it was nothing other than horrendous.


I was trapped within my exploding emotions.

The helplessness which plummeted down on to my shoulders put me into a sphere of bitterness, hatred and revenge.

Three very evil emotions and yes, I was drowning in them.

As I have mentioned I was brought up in a Christian household, with Christian morals, I would say my prayers at night, before going to bed, and I would pray to God, but did saying my prayers make me a Christian?

I did believe in God, or something out there, for hadn't he answered my prayers sometimes as a child. I had been told if you want something bad enough ask God for it, I hadn't been told I was to give love to my maker as well, this had never been mentioned.

At the time I was only using God, what a revelation, isn't that awful? I was using God, and people, not things; I loved things, not people.

How misguided a non believer can be, there was a path for me to follow, it was before me, I was on my walk to God.

I was to suffer accusations, persecution, desertion and betrayal.

While I was suffering this I was sinking deeper and deeper, into a pit of despair.

I wallowed in self-destruction, swallowing the overly emphasised accusations of people who accused me of a crime. How God must have grieved for me!

I let these accusations like dirty water pour over me.

In the middle eighties I wrote a book about knitting, a pattern book which was published.

This book actually found favour at the Frankfurt Book Fair, and surprised me no end. What an achievement.

It was entirely original, and totally my own creations. I had read many books on knitting, but never found what I was looking for, a book which would help the young and new knitters. This being the case I decided to take the initiative, and write one myself.

Going back to when I left school, I worked in a guesthouse which was a short distance from my home. I never had a thought of where this would lead me, or what I would achieve from it. It was the first steps towards the accomplishment of publishing a knitting book, and this step in my life had already been taken.

In my later teens I was given the opportunity to work in a woollen mill. The head designer was a little Jewish man, whom I had already met him, he had been a guest at the guesthouse while I was working there.

Something to be marvel at is our destiny it has already been planned by God Himself; He already knew what experiences I would eventually go through, and where those experiences were going to lead me.

He knew! I really shouldn't be surprised here, with God planning our lives anything can happen; my books I pray will always give Glory to Him. Even if there is a battle to have your book out in the world, don't be disheartened this could mean it needs to be.

Listen to this; I was taught by this little Jewish man who had seen some of my handcrafts, to be simplistic with my designs, for he said, 'simplicity is beauty'. To me this describes so many things in my life.

All the knitting techniques he taught me have been very valuable over the years, for both my writing, and my teaching of handcrafts.

It was in the late eighties and after I had collected enough new designs to write another book, on a new concept in knitting for learners, I had taken my first designs a step further, still staying simplistic though.

I submitted my proposal to a publisher who accepted it; and all my designs which were totally original, they became a knitting book for new knitters for the making of garments. For the experienced knitters who have knitted for many years they may well find it too simplistic for them.

I knit without a pattern as I like to design as I knit.

With this acceptance I had to then put all the notes and the patterns into order. No mean task. Throughout the writing of this knitting book I went out demonstrating the patterns.

It is easy to design something new, but it is a challenge to teach the public to acknowledge your work and believe in it.

I became involved with a committee who practised the art of the very subject in theory close to the book I myself had written about, this being handcrafts, a subject I had been teaching on a much wider scale, for years.

I disclosed the fact I was going to promote my book in Britain the following year, so maybe I would be able to speak about their work in, conjunction with my own book, take heed, I don't advise anyone to do this for there are conflicting interests.

For a few months I went overseas on my trip, and while I was away, as with many committees there were changes, the most obvious being in leadership.

Nowadays some committees do not have elections, who will follow in the leadership position will already be chosen by the minority, this is done whether it is the majorities wish or not, and can be a bone of contention with many people within the structure of the overall committee.

Stick to elections if you can for everything stays in the right order. And the balance will be there for good relationships within the committee structure.

What happens within these changes as the old broom goes out the door, forgive the phraseology, so do all the old ideas, and in my case verbal agreements. With new brooms new ideas came and the old were sweep wide and far.

This is a fact of life.

Now we have the crunch, while I was away on this trip there were a few (at the time I was in complete ignorance to this) who believed I had done a wrong, and as they were the voice, they made it public.

The accusation was I had misappropriated funds for my own use.

The tactics which were employed over the following year were very distasteful.

There will always be someone who will feed the accusers.

All the items concerning this committee were taken from my home without a-by-your leave from my mother or husband.

I do understand the removal made of material concerning the committee, but will never understand the removal of anything else which didn't.

On reflection correspondence travelling from lawyer to lawyer, had comments only known to me written in them.

It was very hard to understand, but I did eventually, I will say here and now my husband and mother never forgave the people concerned. Also they felt their hospitality was abused.

To get over something like this is very hard, but it can be done through forgiveness I have forgiven, not forgotten though. I have God's help in this area.

Forgiveness didn't happened over night it took several months, and I have at last, and the pain I suffered has opened a beautiful path for me.

God has used it for His Glory, and I know **I** will only hurt **me** again if I activate any thoughts concerning these people.

With my commitment to God I promised to love my neighbour.


When I returned from my trip, I returned to a world of snubs and accusations.

Accusations are people making judgements.

Those who judge anyone are themselves judged with the same measure they have judged.


## *Matthew 7:1-2 CEV*

*Don't condemn others, and God won't condemn you. God will be as hard on you as you are on others! He will treat you exactly as you treat them.*

I have learnt people have short memories especially when someone is down in the pits, for they never remember the good about anyone, somehow it is easier to always remember someone's mistakes. This is very sad, but it is the way of the world.

Questions were asked, and investigations.

Ones character is analysed and both sides are questioned, the accused, and the accusers.

Of course who best to ask, than, the people you have tutored, and those you have worked with?

Now I want to cry, I had given them my all, everything I did was done on a voluntary basis. I must have gone astray somewhere for these people were unable to think of anything positive, they were derogatory, very cruel, some of the comments which came back to me, bordered on slander. Many times I was advised to counter balance the cruel remarks.

I remembered though once words are out of your mouth and in the air they can never be retracted. Never utter anything before God if you know it is wrong.

I had to keep on telling myself the following.

God knows me, He is in control, and He evens the score! A song I like says, "He walked a mile in my shoes."

Trouble has beset some of those who accused me, and I have mused on it.

I am now in a safe place, what can man do to me?

I know this, for at a meeting of ministry healing I was given these words; 'I have put you in a safe place, where no one can hurt you again'.

I hold on to that, and I will never let those words go. Hallelujah.

I hold on to the following two scriptures as well.

### *Isaiah 54:9B-10 CEV and Psalm 91:11-12CEV*

We have a choice, whether to ask God into our hearts, or not. I am grateful to have Him in mine, and grateful for making the choice in doing so.

Let me say the alternative is not a pretty life; the worldly situations which are going on around make me want to sing with a 'thankful heart', a line also from a song I like.

Although some of my accusers, are often in my sight, I can say hello them, but something I am thankful for, I do not have to socialise with them.

This began the weeding of unnecessary complications.

The shunning of me was no half affair, it was total, and no one wanted to know me and they certainly wouldn't speak to me.

It was through the power of prayer many people were put in my pathway, and I did get references in my favour, and they were the truth, there was nothing prefabricated, remembering this has made me very humble and I bow my head, for at the time this actually happened I was totally unaware of my spiritual life.

The God I know now, love and owe each day to I believe gave me those references, Hallelujah.

When we are available for anyone at anytime this doesn't automatically mean it will be the same for you.

The worldly life doesn't work like that. Man only sees what he wants to.

You must take the initiative and make the decision yourself, instead of going with the flow of the world agreeing with everyone, or what has been written about you or someone in media reports etc, for there is only one being who knows the truth about anything as well or about anyone, and it is not you.

God never changes, and He certainly will never change what He knows about someone, why should He, for it was Him who created us?

The hatred I was feeling was so intense I was becoming a very bitter person; I was also coming to the stage when I wanted to spill the beans on lives who had confided their innermost secrets to me, especially those concerned in all my hurt and I went through a patch of why should I care about them? I didn't say anything then, and I still haven't.

I had so much to say, but there was something stopping me from speaking out. It never entered my head to be cruel, and my heart was not seeking revenge. I did not want to lower myself to a level of cruelty for it can ruin the speaker by coming back and biting them

Of course I was totally unaware of the power of God, which is mightier than the sword. And yes, 'through my trauma, for it was a trauma, one which my hubby had to go through as well, but he, my Mother some of my cousins whom I had grown up with never stopped loving me and they never once stopped giving me their support.

This meant so much to me and has increased my awareness of love, for another as well as loyalty.

There were others also who stood by me and believed in me, although they didn't understand what it was all about.

**Now we have come to desertion**, which is another thing altogether, for one feels there is nowhere to go; this was certainly true where I was concerned. I had been deserted by some family, whom I always thought were friends. The desertion was through not understanding what was happening, and believing what was read in the papers.

There were bitter moments when many people whom I thought longstanding friends turned their backs on me.

Thinking about this now I question were they my friends?

The answer is no they weren't, and I Praise the Lord, for He has removed these people, I don't need them, God is in my heart, and unseen, He is Spiritual, and in the natural I had my hubby, who is visible a friend and stood beside me all the way.


*__Proverbs 18:10 CEV__*

*__The Lord is a mighty tower, where his people can run for safety__*

Family pride can do a lot of damage; I am talking here about our worldly family; for certainly worldly pride is a sin.

It isn't what one does;

*__Proverbs 17:17 CEV__*

*__A friend is always a friend, and relatives are born to share our troubles.__*

I read once it is the tone of our voice which impresses, not the contract we have landed.

I like that, I have many times told my children it is not what they say it is the way they say it, and this basically is the same thing.

My dearest then care for the way I listen rather than the way I look. Man looks at what is on the outside, and God looks into our hearts.

God loves us, as we are.

This helps me control my thoughts in private.

**Judge not,** I had been judged by many who gave no thought to what would happen once the storm had passed.

I have just witnessed a hail storm, and somehow there seems to be a similarity in the situation for looking out at my garden there has been a cleansing, there has been a lot of growth shredded off the plants, they can now re-grow without the unnecessary growth which was robbing the goodness from the main plant, something familiar there?

I really loathed what I went through from the family I had married into, all the unpredictable things which happened; they were my judge and jury.

Being excluded from family invitations was an insult, it insulted my hubby not just me, he had married me, and he was so kind and tried to take my pain. He was always telling me 'It was lack of understanding which made them like they were'. He knew they would let him down, he said as much, not only through the trauma, also through his illness as well. He had more understanding of his family than they ever realised.

To see someone in their last days isn't really as important, as when they need companionship while alive.

Some visited, but never offered to help us and only one, did so in twenty two years.

God blessed me when He chose my husband, for he was a beautiful man. Hallelujah.

God worked with him to help me through many situations like the one I have just written about and he always had a quiet word of wisdom for me.

Please remember I myself didn't have God in my heart at this time, but God was looking after me through the power of prayer. Hallelujah.

I know jealousy is a sin, so is hatred, and we are told to love our neighbours and this includes our brother or sister.

I know family rejecting is still there today, fortunately it isn't my problem the ones doing it are only hurting themselves. It goes further than me now, for we are a family of numbers, sad! Please don't let it happen to you.

I am writing this for you to see how easy it is to go astray as there are so many different ways to do so.

Do not dislike anyone to the point of rejecting them.

For in reality you only hurt yourself, whether they are guilty or not of what you think. Any civilised purveyor of justice would give you the right to face those who are your accusers! We are told to love our enemies, it takes a strong person to do this, but if we have God in our hearts he replaces hurt with love.

I have had my time to hate, a time to war, and now is my time for peace.

### *Ecclesiastes 3:17 CEV*

*So I told myself that God has set a time and a place for everything. He will judge everyone the wicked and the good.*

We must love everyone all the time.

*Counsel is mine and sound wisdom, I understand, I have strength.*

The world I now entered into with my eyes open, showed me nothing more than what I wanted to see, and this world was the social world.

This is a very pretentious, shallow world.

I found very little sincerity in it; everyone was stepping on the other to reach the top of the ladder.

Where do you go when you reach the top of the ladder?

Unless, you are prepared to come down again, and very few people want to climb to the top and come down again without being awarded, the 'I am great medal'.

You see while you are at the top, and don't forget this; someone is planning to take your place. Tough but true!

This is done usually with the undermining methods of becoming popular with the crowd, becoming indispensable, and they always want to be seen.

You will never be happy at the top unless you like being lonely.

What you have share, give, be there to help others to learn from your knowledge.

Trying to be perfect is a complete waste of time. Some of our achievements we may have perfected, but there is no way we will ever accomplish perfection in ourselves.

There is no perfect person, everyone has a flaw.

If you think this is wrong think on this.

Have you ever committed the sin of omission?

Have you ever failed to help someone, because you might lose your place at the top?

And of what?

Your position is really worthless unless you have been put there by a Higher Authority.

Who ever and wherever you are.

Has your selfishness let you forsake someone in need?

If so you have committed the sin of omission!

Omission is a sin, in the eyes of God.

I was unaware of how many sins we can commit in daytime.

I once read a book which was to put everything into a new light about sin.

A book which is a must to read if you haven't already, it is 'Reclaiming Friendship' By Ajith Fernando, Published by Inter Varsity Press, Leicester England, 1992

The author has used the book of Proverbs from the Bible and simplified it so we can have easy understanding of each chapter. In Part Five of that book, we are told quite bluntly about the sin of omission. The author has done nothing other than give you God's confirmation on the sins we can commit in a lifetime.

### *Proverbs 15:10 CEV*

***If you turn from the right way, you will be punished; if you refuse correction, you will die.***

Messages from the Bible can be described as blunt, what better way to learn though for this way we are able to understand and in understanding we can do and say things with simplicity. It is also repetitive like I am being.

We do not have to complicate our lives, just be simplistic. It isn't a flaw.

I was arrested for fraud, and this really threw me. I had a few agonising days for my arrest was in the middle of the week, how much torture can a person endure?

Plenty, I know.

I had to wait until the following Monday for my first court appearance they were only once a fortnight in this area.

The media had already printed a woman author had been arrested, and as always with the media, there is a pointing finger, not always, I must say, pointing at the right person. Although being an author narrowed it down somewhat, and certainly did in my case.

I was advised to plead not guilty at this appearance.

If I thought I was in another world before my arrest, I didn't know anything, I wasn't ready for the world of revenge, and hatred I was now thrown into. It was so evil; I was being thrown about like a ball, people wanted to throw me to the lions.

The power of prayer was very strong around me, and this was thwarting the enemy for I was still rising up after each blow.

In the New Testament it says 'he who does not believe is condemned'. It was my own lack of faith holding me down, I NEEDED GOD.

And I didn't know Him in his fullness. It was just as well there were prayer intercessors standing in the gap between my accusers and me. This makes me feel very humble, and I will never ever underestimate the power of prayer, it is powerful!

Have you ever seen the sailor's hornpipe danced, where they are drawing the ropes in, well the other night at a Christian meeting I discovered another meaning for this movement, God was drawing me closer to Him, and as I was slowly moving towards Him he was moulding me, into the person He wanted me to be, the person He had planned at the very beginning of my existence in His thoughts.

My education wasn't over yet for there were still many weeks to go before it was finished, and before I was to throw myself at God yelling

"Please help me, please hear my plea, come to me and get me out of this mess. Please God, Oh please God"

I know all the pain I suffered was a learning process. Nobody knew how deep I had driven this hurt into myself, there was many who knew what had been said and done to me, but nobody knew what I had done to me, how it was affecting me personally, and as I felt then nobody really cared.

A good way to put someone down is to cover him or her with mud, learn this and be careful, for mud does dry and it then will brush off. It can leave the thrower then becoming covered with what he threw.

### John15:16 CEV

*You didn't choose me. I chose you and sent you out to produce fruit, the kind of fruit that will last. Then the Father will give you whatever you ask for in my name.*

### 2 Timothy 2:3CEV

*As a good soldier of Christ Jesus you must endure your share of suffering. Verse 7. If you keep in mind what I have told you, the Lord will help you understand completely.*

For me as a disciple I have had firsthand experience on hardship, so I can speak with knowledge about it.

After my arrest, being a writer or author, whichever title you use, the latter has the definition 'anyone who originates something' and the former is defined as 'a person who writes anything that has been written.' My first books have all been originated from my imagination and this story well of course my memoirs are original and yes, I have used other printed sources. Anyway whichever title you want to use, once I was arrested I became a target for the media. They were being spoon fed by a few people who had their own reasons for persecuting me. This persecution went on through the court hearings and for sometime after.

The media write-ups were based on malice and pure speculation. Writing can bring beauty, it can also bring the exact opposite, look up the antonym of beauty sometime, and you will find words like ugly and unpleasantness.

A readily available confidential report was compiled about me; this came from the committee I worked voluntarily with. The availability of this report made it non-confidential, there were many copies which came my way and to many others.

This report had to be read by lawyers as well as others who have professions of very prestigious reputation, these readers, were aghast at how spitefully it had been written, the overall reaction to it was shock.

I was given advice to counter balance the liable and slanderous remarks. There was no need for me to do that, it had been done the moment the words left the writers mouth and pen. I am so thankful I was the reader and not the writer, what a burden to put upon one!

There were also many other things written to me from the same source, I received these on my return from Britain.

First there was a letter stating quite categorically my presence was no longer acceptable to the group, I didn't understand this at the time.

There was the order, 'under no circumstances was I to contact anyone concerned with the committee, I was set up by a few, as what the Bible says, 'there is only need for one scapegoat', in each situation.

We also have from the Bible in Corinthians the same part that I received my authorisation for the writing of this book,

## *2 Corinthians 8:13 CEV*

**I am not trying to make life easier for others by making life harder for you..**

*We are told that Paul was appointed for his work of handling the churches finances along with three others. How wonderful of God, to stop suspicion, as well as criticism. There were three others in the know with him.*

To know humans so well, He gave Paul this protection!

This may be why we always have two or three signatories on cheques and documents?

There were many statements printed quoting me as having said this or that, on my return.

Well, whom did I speak to? The information was never given to me for as I have already mentioned nobody would look at me let alone speak to me.

I was so lonely when I came home; I am now able to understand the difference in having God with you, or to be without Him. My loneliness was almost unbearable; I wonder if you know what loneliness is? Your world collapses. Being on your own doesn't necessarily mean you will be lonely. That can be from choice. My loneliness was more from not knowing God than anything else, for I needed Godly love. God was grieving for me, waiting for me to surrender to Him then He would be able to give me His all.

It is very sad, for out there in the big wide world there are sinners who are very lonely. If you do not walk with God, if you do not know him and have not committed to him, you are walking with his enemy, and that is the devil.

It doesn't matter what you have done, God loves you, he calls for you to come to him to receive salvation, it is then you can ask for His forgiveness, as soon as you have asked, He has forgiven. He knows exactly what you need. If you do not ask you will be forever searching for something.

Without God's love we are a target for all negative thoughts, thoughts we allow to filter through into your minds, letting Satan have a field day with us. I went through all of that so I know what I am saying is true. There are many things that we will do; one is to go to the cake tins eating.

Eating, and eating trying to blot out all your thoughts, trying to become an invisible person, there are some of us who will start to smoke, some of us will drink, there are so many evil vices, I could spend all day naming them and not finish, but you will know what they are just as well as me.

I myself was consumed with evil thoughts don't you doubt it, fortunately I'm not one for going to the cake tins, I don't smoke or drink, but I was lonely.

This is an understatement; one has to have been there to really understand what depths loneliness can put you.

Imagine how Jesus felt when He was on the Cross, thinking He was alone.

For in reality he was, no one wanted to know him.

There were quotations printed by the media as having been said by me, they were false, and they never came from my mouth. I did hear someone say them though!

### *Matthew 18:21 CEV*

*Peter asked Jesus 'how many times should I forgive someone who does something wrong to me? Is seven times enough'?*

*Jesus answered, 'not just 7 times but 77 times'.*

Accusation and desertion are very unpleasant. But it doesn't come near persecution, for persecution is personal.

What I endured was very nasty and eventually through it my rational thought was thrown completely out of proportion.

Persecution is evil, venomous.

When someone deserts you, you know who they are, they have a face and name.

This isn't the way of persecution it can get to you, it can come from anywhere and as always the unknown has the advantage.

The telephone ringing day and night, and when answered, one would get either a loud slam down in the ear, or some uncouth remark.

Trying the pick up and put down straight away method, seemed to incite the caller to ring again and again.

If anyone else answered the phone they would be put off with some mundane remark which was easy to recognise as being spur of the moment nonsense.

The phone calls in the middle of the night were the most frightening.

You do answer the phone at night though don't you?

There were voices we had never heard, as there were some we knew.

By this time the media sensationalism was coming through loud and clear, there had been a few court hearings, and the media coverage of those feed the public who seemed to be thriving on everything they read.

There was evidence of how much feed people received printed in the gossip columns; some of these had very nasty innuendoes in them.

I believe if you ever want to write something to a paper, about anybody in a court case, be sure you yourself are without sin before you throw stones.

I want to tell others they are not on their own when difficult situations arise, gossip is not good, and can be very damaging. Be careful of your tongue.

As a Christian we know we must forgive, for if we don't, God will not forgive us, there is no argument there, and we couldn't get it plainer?

We must forgive and not use anything said about us to seek revenge. This was hard for me, I was going to go for it hammer and tongs, I believed I had the right to take the measure been dealt to me and return it, but nobody has the right to avenge themselves.

It is a very serious action when someone defames another's character. I have nearly done it myself.

Do not come under the misconception that the devil will leave you alone if you are down, there is no truth in that comment. No it is the devil doing it in the first place through someone who has an axe to grind, and it may not necessarily be you. What happened is you got in the way of their axe grinding. Your family are the ones the devil will use to get at you first, as I have found out twice now, I am very grateful for the love of God, and a silent tongue.

With this knowledge I have had the reins pulled in, I have found God has full control of this book, some of my old notes are not needed and some of them are worded differently

Even now as I do revision by request I am writing with love in my heart. Praise the Lord. For over the last few years I have received prayerful healings, a Christian will understand what I have just written, also I have matured with God, and at last there is Godly wisdom coming through. Praise the Lord.

The short time I was to work with this committee, I have found it to be of tremendous benefit to me, I learnt several things that have helped me with my writing and I have become passably proficient at it, I learnt something which is valuable, and this is to be impartial over some comments, being clever with words doesn't necessarily mean a reader will have the same interpretation as the writer. The Bible doesn't play with words God has seen to that, if you do not get the message in the first Part it will be in the next, and the next and maybe the next, if it hasn't reached you wham bam it will be in the next chapter, and even the next keep reading you will get the key (the revelation).


Slowly I was becoming paranoid by everything which was going on around me.

I lived beside a main road and every car was a threat, I thought all of them slowed down when they went by. Not only was I being persecuted by the public, my own imagination was also persecuting me. And this is dangerous.

I changed all the curtains in the house I was able to look out nobody could look in. I was by now anyway a social outcast, if you like a leper. When I look back at this I was becoming almost mentally unbalanced.

I was to suffer acute stress and if you have a need to lose weight what better way than stress, I didn't need to but I did. I was unable to eat.

I have made up for it since though!

I never once turned to God while all this was going on; I was so besotted with the idea I could go it alone. Each time I said this along would come another bomb.

The time for the darkness to become eternal light was drawing closer though. My suffering was going to make me a better person. Yes my suffering was going to make me a person who now is able to help others who have the pain of rejection to cope with.

Rejection was also added to the many things I was to suffer, it is different from desertion, which is to abandon. Rejection is to dismiss, there is a very fine line here, but they are different. Many saw the changes in my lifestyle as guilt, but they were nothing other than self-preservation. You stand in a crowd of people who are all looking anywhere but at you, after a while you will feel as if you are different. Now as a Christian I want everyone to know, I'm not the same, I AM DIFFERENT.

Halfway through my court appearances I changed my plea to guilty, when you plead guilty you become just that, guilty of everything said against you, it no longer matters what the truth is.

This happened the day I was hit with a sledgehammer, well that's what it felt like.

In court the lawyer who was supposed to be defending me was speaking when suddenly there was a loud snort of disgust, this was when I came out of the numbness which I had surrounded myself in, and actually looked at the spectators for this is what they were, I wished I hadn't for there sitting with my accusers, was someone whom I thought was a good friend, a real friend, someone whom I had shared many really happy times with. I felt physically sick at this betrayal.

To know others were gloating over this situation was bad enough, but this person?

Oh no please let it be a mistake.

I looked again, it was real and true, and this friend was sneering at me.

I had hit rock bottom I felt as if I had hit a brick wall.

I commiserate with anyone who through legal aid gets a lawyer who hasn't a clue where you are coming from.

It was after this court hearing I changed my plea. The media had printed I was guilty, the public believed I was guilty, what was left, they might as well have my cloak as well.

I had been shown cheques which certainly had my own, and two other signatures on them. Yes, I must have been guilty. Once the plea was out the truth was of no consequence. Who wanted to know anyway?

It now was an ordeal for me to walk down the street; I felt as if everyone was staring, pointing at me, for the media had certainly excelled themselves. Dad use to say "you only know people are looking at you if you are looking at them."

He was right.

"Big deal" this didn't help me at all. I wasn't able to rationalise any more. The treatment I received in shops was very cruel, I knew most of these people, but they didn't want to know me. Some even told me they didn't want me in their shop. The problem was not mine it was theirs, for they had become my judge and jury; this is a failure with so many people.

I have been judged since the court hearings by many all with their own reasons for doing so. If you are a Christian you can speak nothing other than the truth, you will not have to say you are one, also you will be recognized by your fruits, and being destructive to a fellow Christian, is not of God. We build up a sister or brother we do not try to destroy them.

Society rules how someone is treated, in the worldly realm.

I wasn't having eye contact with anyone on the streets, no doubt in doing this I will have snubbed someone, but my hurt was so deep all I wanted to do was protect me.

Over the betrayal of friends, I would sob my heart out. Sobbing didn't take the pain away though.

Would my life ever be the same? Well who would want it to be if it was going to be like that again?

I never contemplated anything other than to fight, but where had all my weapons gone to?

With the change of plea, things did change though. My accusers were jubilant; they couldn't wait for my sentence. Once I was in jail, they would be able to breathe easier; I wouldn't be able to incriminate anyone.

I never, at anytime cast aspersions on my accusers. But I had a tremendous hatred for them. This is I suppose an aspersion.

### *1Peter 2: 23 CEV*

***Although he was abused, he never tried to get even. And when he suffered, he made no threats. Instead, he had faith in God who judges fairly***

Defining this, "***when they hurled their insults at Christ Jesus, He did not retaliate; when he suffered He made no threats.***

Jesus was my guide although I was unaware of Him being my example. How could I do otherwise?

There were now two hearings to go, and at the second last one, I changed my plea back to not guilty. I wasn't being smart I was playing the system; it was there, to use. When I vacated my guilty plea, this caused a panic, but I had the time I needed, I had no plan in doing this until the very last moment, one judge was quoted as saying 'this case is becoming outrageous'. Little did he know?

There were so many lessons for me to learn throughout the court hearings, not only about those around me, but about myself as well. All of these lessons have come to be very useful over the following years, especially in what I have since worked at and as I healed I was able to take a serious look at myself with a wiser and trouble free heart I have become rather sceptical in my dealings with professionals. There were some professionals who actually denied they had ever worked for me. It didn't matter I had receipts for monies received from me to pay for their services.

Gods knows about this so I will leave it to Him, He will do what is right, and if I am to stay away from these people He will see it happens. Judgement day is in front of us.

<u>*Ecclesiastes 5:8*</u> *CEV*

***Don't be surprised if the poor of your country are abused, and injustice takes place of justice. After all, the lower officials must do what the higher ones order them to do.***

Praise the Lord.

There are some professionals though who are genuinely concerned for others, and not the money they make at the end of the day.

I have had dealings with these also; we must remember these dealings can be misconstrued if taken up the wrong way or by the wrong people.

While the court hearings were going on nobody seemed to want anything concerning verbal or written details which would have made things void.

It was better to look at the situation on the surface as a whole, it also sounded *better and looked good on paper.*

We are told in the Bible, <u>***Matthew 19:24 CEV***</u> ***It is 'easier for a camel to go through the eye of a needle than a rich person to get into God's Kingdom'.*** Money is referred to as 'filthy lucre' and then we are told not to be greedy of it, the other reference to money <u>***1 Timothy 6:10 CEV***</u>*' **The love of money causes all kinds of trouble. Some people want money so much that they have given up their faith and caused themselves a lot of pain.***

This was what my court case was about money, not people.

But it had become unstuck somewhere.

It was a court case about me, it had become very personal, created from jealousy and hatred, but the root of it all was the love of money.

God wants everyone to be wealthy, not necessarily with money though, if they are blest this way it must be honestly toiled for.

There are many people who are blessed by God; for they use their wealth discreetly they do not exploit their riches.

There are those who support charitable purposes, these are in accordance with God's approval. Not letting the left hand know what the right one is doing. Use money, do not love it.

Same thing here, use things not people, love people not things.

As the days go by another month goes by and at last we have come to the end of my court hearings, this part of my life is nearly at an end.

It has been the strangest six months I have ever experienced; there has been so much learning since it. I have had to learn to trust again, as well as see people for what they themselves are, not what I wanted them to be, or they want to be.

I had to change my attitude for sure this is what was needed. It was at the end of a year when I was sentenced; I had vacated my not guilty plea back to guilty, for the time I wanted had been granted to me.

My sentence was six months periodic detention and twelve months supervision.

I had excellent representation and I will always be grateful for all the help I was given, there were many, many people standing beside me now, the reason is so exciting I can hardly wait to tell you about it.

In the time span between the last two court hearings, I had to come to terms with saying I was guilty, although I knew I was saying I was guilty only to my signature being on a few cheques, I was going to have to carry the load for all the accusations.

I was told I should never have pleaded the way I did; there are those who know my plea actually saved them from going through what I did. We can live in a world with a maybe it did but maybe it didn't.

What I did, I did.

Now today the reason for this has become nothing.

I have a friend that is always with me not in my head, but in my heart. This friend will never judge me.

## *Psalm 22:5 CEV*

*When they cried out for help, you saved them, and you didn't let them down when they depended on you.*

After my arrest in July I had become so paranoid I wasn't letting anyone near me and I had become a rather snappy person. My husband worked very hard and certainly didn't deserve any unrest. We had a serious discussion and I moved out to a caravan park away, from my home and him. This move came with a great deal of comment, and there were many who delighted in. "He had thrown her out of the home".

Many others had their own misconstruction for this move. There is nobody who can take from my hubby and I the love we have for one another. This love is what we have built our marriage on. Throughout this situation I never once heard my hubby say one hurtful word to me; he kept on loving and protecting as well as supporting me.

Many people do not understand a love like this, but I will tell you again my husband was chosen for me before either of us was born, it was by the hand of God I was given this wonderful person, and I loved him. Although be honest here you can, and do grump at him! This doesn't stop my loving him though.

I was to believe I had received a message from God telling me to write my story, and this stayed with me, I didn't have any doubts I could write the story, I had doubts about the message I had been given from the Scriptures;

I didn't see it as an authorisation.

I didn't understand.

There was a contradiction of emotions going on in me, I was writing up a draft as fast as I could, but didn't have the drive to keep going.

I will tell you now my first notes have all been used in this book.

God moves in a mysterious way!

Then once again a year later I was to receive the same Scripture, ah but now I was in a different realm, I was spiritually filled, I was 'born again'.

A healing had taken place in my body, a healing which let me know I was receiving the 'Word of God'. Also there were three witnesses.

All the negative feelings I had were turning into positive feelings. Each one of my burdens which had been holding me down, began slowly to disappear, I have just thought of an analogy, We have a blown up balloon and when it explodes it isn't there any more, this was what my problems had become as I passed them on to the Lord they burst into nothing. Sometimes I would pass over a burden and immediately take it back. I was learning to trust God, but at the time and while I was doing it I was only trusting 80%. And each time I took a burden back, I was the only one hurting.

Nobody but God knew what was going on.

Gradually, as I released all my burdens, I found I was trusting 100%.

This was about the time I received the Scripture again about my writing and it was exactly the same, word for word.

## 2Corinthians 8:10-11 CEV

*A year ago you were the first ones to give, and you gave because you wanted to,*

*So listen to my advice. I think you should finish what you started.*

I am very thankful my attitude had changed; I actually understood it this time.

I went into a furore of writing more notes. I had so many by this time, I thought they were the book; all I would have to do was collate them. Dream on it isn't that easy!

The day I committed myself to God and was filled with the Holy Spirit, I just simply accepted I was saved, totally. I have never since denied Jesus; I have never doubted the beauty of the Lord's ways. The beautiful life He has planned for me, I feel so happy so contented, and oh so loved by my Father in Heaven, through Jesus Christ.

Only the Lord can give us the peace I have.

I have never doubted God would help me when I asked for his help, but there have been many times when I have received an answer I didn't expect. I once read ' God's answers are wiser than our prayers'.

This is a very profound statement one we should remember. It helped me to understand the following

***Isaiah 55:8, 9 CEV***

***The Lord says: 'My thoughts and my ways are not like yours.***

***Just as the heavens are higher than the earth, my thoughts and my ways are higher than yours'.***

Jesus died on the Cross for us; and we mustn't let this horrendous event be for nothing.

Think about this. Who should have died on the Cross?

It should have been me and yes you! Sinner I was. Jesus never did a wrong deed in his short life! He died for us, what a sacrifice.

I have picked up my Cross, I don't drag it, I carry it and I try to stay humble.

I wear a Silver Star of David around my neck, there are many who say it is only an ornament, and they are right with the superficial appearance of it, but for me personally it has two symbolic meanings, it symbolises death for when I offered myself to God the old me died. There is confirmation for us in the Bible, the book of ***Matthew 16:34*.CEV** as there are other references to this in the New Testament. There is one that I dearly like and could apply to this book,

***1Corinthians 1:17* CEV Christ *did not send me to baptise. He sent me to tell the Good News without using big words that would make the cross of Christ lose its power.***

Then we have the second reason, my Cross keeps me humble. When I get on my high horse and start something I know I am certainly not able to finish, for I don't have all the answers, I suddenly become conscious of my Cross and what it really stands for. The truth here is my spirit has made me conscious of my actions and I back off. For everyone who does wear a Cross they will have their own reasons for it.

Praise the Lord!

Their reasons deserve respect, not criticism.

We also have the Cross as a witness to Jesus.

I have seen people look at mine then they look at me, this actually makes me laugh inwardly for they have acknowledged Jesus without actually knowing it. The wonderful thing is those thoughts are also known to God.

Who knows it might well be their first step towards a life of contentment, a life with God, as their very own Saviour.

It is some years now since I myself received the Holy Spirit and the complete freedom I was promised. I fluctuated from primer one to primer four continually in the learning process of being a Christian Believing Believer.

God knows all of us, believers and non-believers, he knows everything we need, and it is only Him who clears and makes the path for those things to be corrected. How beautiful?

I get excited every time I see a rainbow, for this keeps me in good stead for the day or hours ahead of me. Some of us do need visible signs and there is nothing wrong wanting this, if our hearts are free, we will see these signs as nothing other than a personal 'hello' from God. The rainbow tells me God will always keep His promises, for it has been written and can be found in our book the Holy Bible.

I love my own personal relationship with my Father in Heaven.

The hurt I carried inside of me was making me ill, and I started to shut myself off from everyone especially my husband, in doing this I was hurting him. Communication is a very important part of marriage, the lack of it can lead to conflict, hostility and then there are arguments. There will be words said and once they have been spoken they can never be retrieved, he who utters is heard.

Do you realise WHAT I am saying everything we say before God is heard EVERYTHING. I know with this revelation there will be many who are shuddering for what they know they have said.

Just as I know there will be many who wish they had said more. I have learnt now **to listen to what I say,** and am now stopping mid sentence, for if I say I don't want to …this or that I know now I will be doing this very thing sooner that later. God loves us, He loves us to be aware He has ordained us to be where He wants us and we may find, this place is where we don't want to be, and have said so in careless conversation.

My husband has a quiet sense of humour, which I thoroughly enjoy; as well he has a brilliant intellect. Like many intellects he isn't always practical, but in our family each one of us loves and supports him. The times I heard the boys putting him right showing him his head can help his legs, by taking a short cut, they did this with the same kindness he gave them when they were young, learning things on the farm. Life has turned a full circle for them.

The people who didn't know I had moved out of my home were soon put in the know. The media were on to it as it was mentioned in one of the court sessions. My understanding of court sessions can not be written for there are no words to describe how I feel about them, there are many cases heard through a day, and the waiting isn't pleasant, 'everyone stares'. Be careful what you do in court this goes for the offenders as well as the visitors, for the judge has ears, and somehow I believe he doesn't miss very much.

Once it was known I had left home I saw many people driving around the park to see if it was true. This didn't help me at all I felt another cruel blow to the torture being put upon me. The caravan I stayed in was near the ablution block and it was over a week before I was able to go there in daylight. I was terrified to leave the van, in case I walked into some danger waiting for me.

My change of address didn't stop the persecution, I was still to get snide remarks as well as sneers, and this continued until well after my court sessions were over. Although it was very real at the time I have wondered since why people, who are not even connected with court cases, can get such a perverse pleasure out of someone's misfortune and the other thing is why papers print the slanderous and derogatory letters sent in.

Living in the caravan I found I was desperately in need for a friend, there were a few who came to see me, I realised as they have never seen me since they were being nosey for once the sentence had been passed there has been no sight of them

In the Apocrypha, and do not confuse this with the book of **Ecclesiastes** in the Old Testament from our Bible

**Ecclesiastics 6:**

*If thou wouldiest get a friend, prove him first do not be hasty to credit him.* **Then also from this book we have, '*forsake not an old friend, for the new is not comparable to him, a new friend is as new wine, when it is old, and thou shalt drink it with pleasure.*'** I have found this also *Envy not the Glory of a sinner, for thou knowest not what shall be his end.* You may dislike the sin, but do not dislike the sinner.

They are very wise verses, whichever one you choose.

My attitude changed me over many things, and I only need as many friends as fingers on one hand. I have God as one, my hubby is another. God has me at peace. Believe this I can and do still get hurt when I see how people get pleasure out of being cruel to another!

We must not be hasty with our praise; this is a misguided misconception, because I thought if I didn't harm anyone, I myself wouldn't get harmed. Early in my trial and my new walk with the Lord I never had enough confidence to trust Him completely, and whenever I received a knock after the court hearing, I would rush to my hubby, he never said so, but he must have sighed sometimes, and wished I would get myself together.

God must have sighed out loud at times too. My hubby said to me 'you have given them more credit than they have given you.' In my daily scripture this morning, I have read 'God has things to teach you every day.' And as this was a day the Lord had made I was to be glad and rejoice in it. Hallelujah.

When I dedicated my life to God, at first I often lost my way; I would forget to pray my problems through. I am not talking about the prayers I have in the morning, my daily talk to God, I am talking about taking my burdens to him instead of putting myself through unnecessary pain, I am talking about complete communication with Him, without leaving anything out. He knows everything and knows what I left out, but will not interfere without my asking. I know this, I know in my Noah (knower). I love that we have a choice, always. We have a choice.

This was something I had to learn. With this complete communication now with God, I have no problems which can not be overcome; I am under his wing, in a safe place. Hallelujah. Why did I think I could manage on my own? Why did I think God needed me to start solving my problems? Why did I think God needed a hand? I will tell you, I needed more faith, Peter was walking on water until he stopped looking at Jesus; and then he started to sink. Yes FAITH is the strength we need. *"Ye of little faith'*, was what Jesus said to Peter. As I grew with God, my understanding of Him and His power also grew I was to see 'His Glory knows no bounds'. And as I learnt not to wallow in self-pity, I was able to go to my Bible and renew my strength from the word and prayers.

There have been many times since my court case, when I felt I was being rejected, it happened to me last week, and the week before and before and before, but it was me, **I** was rejecting **myself**. God will never reject you. He is faithful, He was faithful to me in my past, although I wasn't aware of it, He is faithful to me in the present, and I know He will be faithful to me in the future. Hallelujah.

### *Timothy 2:3* CEV

*As a good soldier of Christ Jesus you must endure your share of suffering. Soldiers on duty don't work at outside jobs. They try only to please their commanding officer.*

Don't misunderstand this, for the Lord will give you understanding in everything. *'Believe me'*. You will know and begin to understand. This will happen when you relinquish your self completely to God.

I had to learn and understand about judgement. I had to recognise it from the point of view as a committed Christian; God was guiding me and everything I did to be in obedience to Him. Did this mean I had to love everyone?

Yes it did. When I stopped loving people I would judge them, coldness would come over me, and then I had to back up to see where I had gone wrong. I had criticised someone, I had seen something in them, but wait, this same flaw was in me, and this is why I noticed it, so back on my knees once again, to repent.

I had to take accountability for my criticism, and take it to the Cross, and by repenting was (is) the only way to be free again.

God can work with me in this area now.

God knows what he is doing; and only He knows why he is doing it. I have let Him control me, and now I am cautious with people, I am no longer a person who gets deluded with beguiling speech. *'I am absent in body, yet I am with you in Spirit,' Jesus said*, I know the Holy Spirit has control.

Here is another way of putting this, as a dedicated Christian Believing Believer, who lives in a human world, 'I am not of it, I have been reborn, and I have dedicated my heart to God as he has wanted me to.' I love God, he is my best friend, and He is my confidant. I try to judge no one, and if do, I can put myself in their shoes and see it from another angle, "God's" and then see how I get on.

I said before not to forsake an old friend, I did have a friend who never once left through my court hearings, she came with me for every hearing, it was another pair of ears.

My friend took me to the Lydia Fellowship meeting where I became a converted Christian. She gave me her support and didn't ask questions. While I was staying in the caravan she called to see me on many occasions and never once made any demands on me. From her I received total acceptance of me as I am, we only need four true friends, for me, one is God, and one was my hubby, do I now have another?

I have often thought she swallowed the book of Proverbs sometime in her life, for she was Godly wise. I did depend on her too much after the court case and this put a strain on our friendship, for a soul tie had developed, very unhealthy and definitely not Godly, there was a dependency on her and not God. With soul ties one lives and breathes the other person. This had to be taken to the Cross to God to be broken I felt so grateful for her being with me all the time when I needed someone, and this was a danger for her and me, I needed her always at my side or so I thought . When the court hearings were all over except the singing, I wanted to follow my own Godly path, but I felt guilty (pardon the pun) for doing so, and this definitely wasn't Godly.

We now go our own ways as individuals' no longer feeling we have to be together. God knows everyone must walk their own walk for He has ordained this. Also he knows the times and speed He wants us to grow.

Many years ago when I was put in the pathway of my friend I felt there was an aura of something surrounding her; I recognised it, and wanted it for myself. Through a day I would go up and down with moods, maybe it is my creative temperament! She never seemed to be any different. When I asked her if she ever got hurt she said 'yes', this actually surprised me, now of course through my Christian growth I can see she is no different to me.

One day when my hubby came to see me I asked him to bring me my Bible, if he was surprised he didn't show it, how do you think I felt after those words had left my mouth?

My reading wasn't very successful though, I didn't know what to read, and what I did read, I didn't understand. **Hold in here though** the first step had been taken. My transformation had started. This was the first step forward. The beginning of my new life was to turn me around and give me release from all my burdens eventually. I was still in the van, still wallowing in self-pity, but the pit wasn't quite so full now, something had happened and things didn't look so black.

Each time she came to see me I could see a light at the end of a tunnel. A pin point of light, and it was growing bigger each day. The ice around my heart which had held me frozen in limbo was starting to melt.

### ***Now the full details from the introduction.***

In the early nineties I was invited me to go with her to a Lydia Fellowship meeting out of town; my answer was 'yes' and this came out of my mouth so fast I didn't even give myself time to weigh it up.

Who was going to be there? I just said I would go. Of course when I was alone I thought 'what have I done, what on earth have I let myself in for?' Then I thought 'what the hec, I have a day to kill,' how blasé, can one get?

The dreaded Saturday came around it was THE DAY before I realised it.

Weatherise the day was sunny and calm. What a pair, you should have seen us. One smiling and happy, me smiling, well my lips were pulled into some position, but I was a sour, very bitter, an empty hearted person.

The first thing I had to face up to was going into a crowd again; the last big crowd I had been at was in Britain at my last demonstration.

Phew! I was in the hall, I had a tag put on me, this time though it actually had my name on it, anyway whatever. I had been labelled; all around me was an air of expectancy, what on earth was going on?

What have I done coming here, I felt as if a time bomb was going to explode.

Little did I know there was something very different for me, I didn't feel threatened, but I will say my insides were turning somersaults?

I was introduced to another woman, who had been praying for me while I was going through my trauma, this was a very humbling experience, for I had the mistaken idea in my mind nobody cared enough about me, and certainly didn't care to pray for me.

I was sitting quietly trying to squeeze myself into a small space; I didn't want to look as conspicuous as I felt.

I didn't want anyone to look at me and think, 'boy has she got a problem.' Of course I was the only one there with problems! Ha! Think about it!

Fellowship meetings are beautiful, the Holy Spirit the Spirit of God comes in and takes over, I saw the careful planning of a very reverent time turn into something almost chaotic. But love for each other filled the hall, and it was very obvious everyone knew they were loved, how I didn't know at the start of the meeting, it was a new experience for me.

***When two or more are gathered God will be in their midst***, so the Bible says.

As I sat with these women, I became aware of the toll the last few months had taken on me, my mental attitude was drowning me, and I wondered if any of these things were visible, could the other women see how sad I was.

Somehow this feeling of sadness was very out of place in this hall.

It was so peaceful; and I could feel the peace, something I hadn't felt for a long time.

The meeting was opened, everyone was welcomed, and then songs of praise to God were sung. This touched my heart the praise was so beautiful, and yes I was joining in.

When we sat down my mind started to wander, I was thinking I never played my music anymore.

Then came another realisation I never laughed spontaneously anymore, I was a happy person before all of this, life was beautiful and I would always manage to get through each day without too many downers.

What was I doing to myself? My sense of humour had completely disappeared.

I was receiving a picture of myself, one I didn't like, I had become the very opposite to what I use to be.

I watched the morning guest speaker rise, be introduced, and I saw her speaking, but my thoughts were miles away.

I was in the past, I was thinking about my children; I was remembering the tricks and games they used to play.

A picture of my second daughter, came into my mind, she was always playing tricks on her siblings. If it wasn't her it would be the first boy. I loved them both for it. They were being themselves.

I suddenly remembered a prank, my hubby and I had bent the rules about bedtime, we let them have a treat.

They went with their father to burn off some stubble after the harvester had been in the paddock. I stayed at the house for some reason but I could hear them laughing and shouting. Suddenly, it was like a hurricane, three children rushed inside looking as if they themselves were on fire.

I loathed it when something like that happened, my imagination would run riot. Eventually one of them was able to tell me their sister had introduced them to the big ugly ogre who lived in the willow trees.

There was very little this ogre couldn't do, I was able to calm them by putting them right about the non-existent ogres anywhere, waiting for the culprit to come in. Who duly arrived, smiling and looking as if nothing had happened, I must say she didn't understand to what length her prank had gone, for it was one rotten disturbed night for me. Three children had nightmares while she slept calmly totally unaware of the disturbance.

All you mothers can smile here, it happens sometimes? Huh

The lassie was reprimanded, and told about laughing at the misfortune of others. She had a little lesson to learn, you have to be able to laugh at yourself, I actually thought she would never make it, maybe she hasn't I will never know, we did come through it at the time by not making too big an issue out of it. ***The quiet voice has more power than the big stick.***


Suddenly I came out of my daydreaming, to hear the speaker say, "Samuel was being called, and Samuel answered, 'Here I am'". Something triggered in me and I felt as if it was me who had said 'Here am I'. This simplicity had caught me and I was listening, I even opened my Bible and found ***Samuel 1:3*.CEV** the theme of the morning's lesson was delivered in simple phrases with confidence, she believed what she was saying, and this started to rub off on to me, as I followed the Bible word for word. I went on a Biblical path with Samuel. Once again I felt the healing peace of God. Even though I still felt as if I had been run over, my heart had been so bitter, but the peace around was covering me, Praise God for His precious peace. I acknowledge the fact I was meant to be in this hall, it had nothing to do with me having a 'day to kill'; I had been guided here for a specific reason.

The feeling of claustrophobia, when I entered the hall had completely gone, and I was starting to enjoy myself. Something was happening to me and it seemed to be happening at a great speed. Over the few hours in the hall I had changed my thoughts from negative to being positive, I found I was unable to hold on to the negative. And I was in a presence. It was awesome, I could feel the peace spreading through my body, and this peace was softening my heart. Even my face muscles were relaxing, and I wanted to hear more.

The morning was really enjoyable, once I started to listen that is, and joining in with the prayers seemed to be the natural thing to do. There were times when I thought the speaker was talking about me, and wondered how she knew this or that, it was at the back of my mind 'I will get someone when we leave.' What I didn't notice as I was sliding down in my seat, many others were doing the same. I found this out later and I felt better, I was no different to them. Praise the Lord.

God had worked through a friend, to bring me to this meeting, for something of great significance was going to happen.

The morning session closed with a perfect ending, for a perfect lesson, with prayers.

Lunch time came and went with a quiet buzz of conversation, as if no one wanted to lose the atmosphere and the presence of the Holy Spirit, for He was certainly there.

Although I still wasn't a (born again) Christian I knew with certainty who was in the hall with us. I felt as if He was smiling at me.

We went for a walk, for of all things my friend wanted to buy a guinea pig. It was strange for when we went outside I felt everything would be different, but it was just the same maybe the sun was brighter, but nothing had changed. There had been a change though, it was in me. Goodness me, at last I was starting to see the light of God by myself, I didn't need anyone to tell me about it.

The feeling of apprehension was still there as we started to go back, half of me wanted to go into the hall, the other half wanted to escape, to go back to the safe zone I knew, although it wasn't a good place to be it was comfortable.

The afternoon lesson started with prayers and songs of praise, and then a new speaker delivered her message. Suddenly I felt as if I was on another planet. I was listening as testimonies to God were being shared; I was stunned with awe at how God had touched these women's lives. It was so beautiful, I silently wished I could have (one would do) an experience like those I was hearing. I really enjoyed the wonderful witnesses.

Then the negative came over me, taking the enjoyment from me. I felt out of my depth, was I good enough for God, was I worthy of God, didn't I have a criminal record?

It was then with absolute certainty in my inner being I knew I needed God, I knew I wanted to serve Him for the rest of my life doing whatever he chose for me.

I knew with certainty I was to write a testimony to Him, for He had ordain it, three times given the words to me.

It wouldn't have been possible with the attitude of self-righteousness I carried, I never thought for one moment this attitude had made me a self egotistical, unapproachable person. When I went to the Cross later in the day, this horrid attitude left me, I dropped it like a red hot poker at the foot of the Cross. I have never regretted doing so and never will.

I have become so rich, through my Godly knowledge. From this knowledge I can share with you the following, God loves us no matter what we have or haven't done; He loves you, He loves me, and yes, He loves us so much he said'.

### *Hebrews 13:5 CEV*

***Don't fall in love with money. Be satisfied with what you have. The Lord has promised that he will not leave us or desert us.***

Isn't that beautiful?

For those who have neglected someone or something, or neglected to go somewhere, God still loves you. I find this so overwhelming. Many times I feel I am going to burst, with this love.

God is in my fingertips as I write to you, my hands are full of love, and they want to spill this love over you as you read. I so want you to know His love and peace.

At the meeting we had prayers for war torn Ireland and once again I went into another sphere. When I received my very first vision from God, I had no idea what to do, but I saw everything so clear I actually thought the people concerned were with me in the hall.

There were three figures, a woman dressed in black with a long hair braid around her head; she was looking at a little girl who had long black hair, and very dark eyes.

Then there was a soldier, he was dressed in a camouflage uniform with a blue beret.

All three of these people were shown to me so clearly I could see their features, I knew I would know them if I ever saw them again.

Although the vision was over very quickly my memory had registered every detail. As God intended it should.

I shared my vision with the others feeling slightly embarrassed, my voice shook as I spoke, but I got there.

As we were praying about Ireland it was taken for granted it was from nowhere else. This turned out to be a wrong assumption of course, but I wasn't to know until two years later.

I was so blessed that Saturday in the early nineties, God had touched me. He had trusted me to do His will, to pray for the people in my vision. This was before I even relinquished myself to him. He knew I would.

I never doubted the validity of this vision. And two years later I was to hear over the radio news about the children and woman. They were in a war torn country and yes my soldier was there as well. When the story was announced over the radio about them I was astounded, I had been praying for two years over my vision. I didn't realise it until at a prayer meeting later that day. I was suddenly to see the soldiers face again, and then I knew it was my soldier.

I knew my vision had come into existence, into being a reality.

Yes! The beret was pale blue worn by the peace Corp. If it had been Ireland like it was thought the soldier would have been wearing the maroon beret, of the paratroopers.

Never mind what ever colour the beret was, I prayed for those in my vision in obedience to God.

It is wise to wait, and listen until God is ready to reveal things to us. I waited, well actually I didn't know what to do, but waiting went well with me.

God trusted me at the time to do exactly what I did and that was pray. I still have in my Bible the newspaper cutting about these people as a reminder, God with his love trusts us for he knows if we walk close to him, we will follow through in obedience to do the work he has set for us.

After the speaker had finished there was an altar call.

Suddenly, I found myself in front of the altar, it sounds really easy doesn't it, but let me tell you it wasn't, there were fights going on inside of me, something was saying go, and something else was saying you don't need to.

Using black and white for comparison, black looks dark unknown, sometimes threatening, where white is light, bright and inviting.

I went up and offered myself to God, I can't remember if anyone came with me I do remember the words of the lady up front asking me to breathe in deeply. And as soon as I did, for a 'beyond words moment' I was somewhere else and my spirit was responding to another spirit, and with this came an absolute belief in my heart the steps I had just taken where the best steps I would ever take in my life.

I was crucified with Jesus Christ, and the old I was dead. Praise God I could now live, and go forward.

I had been reborn, Zap, I was forgiven of all my past sins immediately I uttered my repentance, all the feelings of revenge within me, the hatred I had felt, everything which had made me bitter, all of those were forgiven. The repentance of my past sins was absolute. God didn't have to think about it, for He had known I would be at this meeting and He knew I was going to utter the words, 'Yes Jesus come into my heart have your way with me, I dedicate my future life to you, I am yours.'

I felt a covering of love pour over me as I breathed Jesus into my very being, I felt as if I had put on a very soft coat of love, and this being so I could feel love from my fingertips to my toes.

This love spread through my body from my heart over the next few weeks and the day I was to be sentenced I was a completely new person.

I had been released from all my burdens; they had fallen from my shoulders, and landed at the Cross of Jesus.

I am to remember He took all my sins those of my past and those of my future. The future sins which I had not committed he took and when I activate them for I will fulfil them, I am to repent with sincerity and give them to the forgiving God. They had already been forgiven at the Cross by Jesus.

Through God's love everything was put into proportion, and what I had thought to be 'anthills' were but nothing. My problems became 'what problems'.

Never let problems become an excuse, God never gives you any more than you can endure in a day, there is only one person who can save you.

Our, One True God. You will be disappointed if you think otherwise. It is not me; it is through the power of Jesus Christ. Please hear these words, and understand them with your heart. If you are putting yourself through torture through other peoples ignorance, please don't, please turn to God if you can't see the way out, and even if you can see the light still go to God, give Him your thanks and your love. He knows what you are going through, and will be grieving for you, wanting to help you, but He can only help you, if you invite Him to do so.

I had all the pain of rejection, desertion, accusations, and persecution taken from me by uttering one sentence; everything had vanished into thin air. They became nothing but vapour. Hallelujah.

### Take control of my life

### Make me the kind of person you want me to be

From the moment I surrendered and repented, God immediately saw me as it says in the Bible, faultless and innocent of sin.

To the unbeliever this may sound like nonsense, it is understandable, for didn't we feel the same when we were unbelievers. Believe this when you do believe, and are living in the presence and trusting God, praising Him giving thanks daily to Him, you are going the right way, there will be hiccups, but they can be easily disposed of.

It may take sometime to find this out, but with God guiding us how can we go wrong? Twenty plus years I am still learning from God. As growth continues we become stronger, and with it an easy recognition of the right and wrong way.

We can stop negative thoughts getting a foothold in our lives; there is no place for anything other than the positive in our walk with God.

Everyone will deviate from his or her Godly path, it is inevitable we live in a human world; I did several times, and each time I was able to leap back on to the positive track. I really believe everything that happened to me had to happen as part of my learning.

It took me from my day of commitment until the middle nineties before I found the complete freedom God wanted me to have.

There were a few sharp corners needing to be knocked off. Some of the time I spent screaming for God to give me release over something or other; this could have been too easy, it was me who had to release them to God. There were things which attracted me and were not always Godly, and there were other distractions. While these ungodly things were within me, I would run amok. We need to understand with our hearts everything around us. Satan is in the world, and tries to influence our lives so subtly.

The power of prayer is so powerful, so heed this, and be careful what you utter in the name of Jesus.

I learnt the hard way, I prayed for something which turned out to be a complete disaster, it was to do with my writing and to make it worse I took umbrage at the answer I received.

My request had been totally selfish. I had no need for it, but I sure needed the lesson, and God let it happen.

I know He gives us everything we NEED He will see us fulfilled each day. Ask, believe, and you receive, it is very simple. Don't be like me knowing these things, enjoying the power I had for the wrong reasons, the power Jesus gave us when He departed this earth, power we must never abuse. I had to learn to be more diligent and respectful with this power.

My prayers at this time were for my own self-esteem, I wanted to say, 'ha ha I'm back again', and I wanted to say 'see, so there'. I went through a little refection over this episode, but was soon able to put it behind me by repenting and repent I did, and yes there was a COMPLETE turn around.

God's answers are wiser than our prayers. I had to stop trying to help Him, and let Him have his own way, and His rightful place in my heart. I praise God for His patience with me, and His grace and mercy. I have learnt this, and I don't push the limits… Not always!

Spoken by Jesus, we have one of my favourite scriptures from,

***Luke 10:19-20 CEV** I have given you the power to trample on snakes and scorpions and to defeat the power of your enemy Satan. But don't be happy because evil spirits obey you. Be happy that your names are written in heaven*

## *Acts 16:31 CEV*

*Have faith in the Lord Jesus and you will be saved! This is also true for everyone who lives in your home.*

It was while my friend and I were driving home I suddenly realised that over the last few hours, I hadn't given any thought to my problems. This was amazing I couldn't believe it, my heart was no longer heavy, and the best part was I was unable to bring them and the faces of my accusers into focus; it was only a short time ago since I stood before the altar. Praise the Lord.

## *2 Corinthians 6:1-2,CEV*

*We work together with God, and we beg you to make good use of God's kindness to you. In the scriptures God says, 'When the time came I listened to you, and when you needed help I came to save you." That time has come. This is the day for you to be saved.*

This makes Saturday in the early nineties, the following

*'Behold now is the acceptable time; behold now is the day of salvation'.*

My acceptance of God was total, I had to learn His ways, and by learning these I grew with Him, and learnt to listen, I learnt to see with my heart, I learnt to rest, to wait for God, I learnt not to rush in by myself, to run amok, then scream for Him to bail me out.

He never rushes, He is always on time, and I had to learn everything is in His time. He knows all the suffering I went through, He went through it with me at the Cross, I will endeavour to spend my future working for His Glory, and in doing so I will receive blessings.

This I find awesome, where I had loathed every one of my accusers and everything about them, I was able to love them for God had filled me with His love, and had given me extra so I was able to forgive them.

This forgiving is complete, if they were in strife I wouldn't hesitate to help them, I would be able to do so without question, I would be doing it in obedience to God, for we have been told the second most important commandment is to love our neighbour.

I have to say here though **I am human**, there are many people out there although I would help them, if there was a need, I will never associate personally with them, I will never partake food with the devil, and we have this choice, for we are individuals. Praise the Lord.

I was at the turning point of my life; I had exchanged my convenient God for the God there is, God the all powerful. WOW THAT IS BEAUTIFUL!

I had stopped rejecting Him, and in doing so I was able to draw unto him. The times I asked for help from Him since the Lydia Fellowship meeting are uncountable. At first I didn't recognise some of the answers for they were given to me by His will, not my will. I write again, God's answers are wiser than our prayers. Praise the Lord.

There is so much to learn and understand, and this is why the acceptance of our renewed mind takes us so long to fully understand, each time we accept a new thing in God, we become lighter and brighter people, we are children of His, we are free, and we are realising we have a free spirit. Hallelujah.

We have now reached my sentencing, for it was the perfect time 'The Lord is my helper, I will not fear, what can man do to me?'

I am going in the right direction, to receive and have a peaceful existence. I am looking out of the window and I see, trees standing upright and still, there are cattle just over the stone wall, the ducks are enjoying the sun, so are my doves, they are strutting around the lawn, there is an air of peace out there.

Two nights ago this wasn't the sight I saw, for we had the strongest gale I can remember, it was horrendous, there was so much damage to the trees and garden, I wondered if it would ever be calm again. It is of course, and so am I, for these things are only temporary.

Eventually I arrived back at the caravan; I was exhausted, my day hadn't been physically strenuous, but mentally phew! I just fell onto my bed; my mind for the first time in months was rested.

I read the book of Isaiah, and while I was reading this lovely book, I remembered at home on a wall I had a painting with this verse on it,


'**Isaiah 43:2.CEV**

'*When you cross deep rivers, I will be with you, and you won't drown*'. Suddenly I realised God had been protecting me all of my life. He had been waiting for me. He had always been with me, for everything I experienced had never been too unbearable. Praise the Lord.

There was always a choice for me to see things from two different aspects. God had been with me. I would never have believed it if I had been told. I was, walking around with blinkers on, only seeing what I wanted to.

'*I was blind but now I can see.*'

I read the lesson from Samuel again, and I knew I had been gently led me to the meeting.

God used my situation, my indecision's, and had someone to bring me to Him. Can you see the sailors pulling in the ropes?

The melodrama which followed the second to last court hearing wasn't very nice.

The slanderous comments I heard about myself could have frozen my heart again, but they didn't for I had victory on my side now, and this is all one needs, for what can man do to me I say again? In the days before my sentence I became very strong, and each day I received an added strength, a strength which enabled me to tidy up many details I had been leaving undone.

I was given another chance to 'spill the beans' as the saying goes, for it was obvious now many things were unspoken. For me the time to talk had passed. I was no longer the negative person of yesterday; I had become the positive person I am now. I had acknowledged a supernatural power, which was guiding and protecting me, I was surrounded by this power. Living in the caravan had ceased to be a torment, I found I was able to look at people, look them in the eye, not at their backs as they walked away from me. I did feel threatened sometimes, but would look up towards God. As I keep saying, what can man do, if God is for you who can be against you? And if a dart gets thrown at me, I would put my hand up, which I still do, and it will ricochet back to the sender.

***Forgive me my trespasses as I forgive them that trespassed against me.***

There were many who noticed the difference in me; but didn't know what it was. I had no attitude, all the victimisation which I had bottled up and the hurt within me over the last few months had gone.

I had released my burdens to God. The change in me was a witness to Him. He received the Glory and I received the blessing with both hands. Ever since my commitment I have poured the living words from my Bible into my heart, this has helped me in forgiving anyone who defamed my character, leading people to see me as something other than the true me. There were so many words spoken, and they nearly broke my heart, words coming from mouths in sour grapes, and maybe jealousy from people who had never been in my company or spoken personally to me.

Words saying my handcrafts were shoddy, and not up to standard. Whose standard I have often wondered? I am only too happy to have lessons if my work is brought up a standard of God's acceptance.

There has always been a demand for my crafts; this is still happening, and people still come to me to be taught a craft, I will not stop teaching to help another, for I have been given a gift to share. I do not have to justify myself, my work has brought appraisal and approval all over the world. My capabilities in handcrafts are a gift from God, and I have no need to boast about them.

*Proverbs 27:2* CEV *Don't boast about yourself- let others praise you.*

**Verse 4***: An angry person is dangerous, but a jealous person is even worse.*

The love of the people around me as well as Godly love has shown me anything is possible if we love and believe. It is progressive the journey we walk when following our Lord and Master. Through it we learn to differentiate between the love of God, and the bitter pill Satan can give us. Do not drop the Cross at any time be alert.

The Cross which saved us isn't very heavy, you only need to slip a tissue thin line away from God, and Satan will grab you.

When anyone actually says they don't believe in Satan, I groan inside myself, I will tell you here and now you may not believe in Satan, but he certainly believes in you.

We as Christians are only given as much as we can endure in a day, as I have said many times, for we live one day at a time. When you are in trouble whether it is from your own doing or someone else's, or with your emotions, rest in the Lord, and wait patiently for Him.

You may have to utter words of repentance, or ask forgiveness.

GOD never leaves us, everything is in His timing.

We have come to my last court appearance, I was of light heart, although a little apprehensive. I had certainly attracted a crowd; there wasn't an empty seat in the court room. All the priming up telling me what to expect hadn't actually prepared me for the crowd. I went along with a little Bible in my pocket; I had on my Spiritual Armour,

*The **Armour of God**,*

*The **Belt of Truth**,*

*The **Breastplate of Righteousness**,*

*The **Shoes of Peace**, which is the word of the **Gospel**,*

*A **Shield of Faith**,*

*The **Helmet of Salvation**, and*

*The **Sword of the Spirit** in my hand all invisible, but with me.*

I knew what the verdict was going to be. But this didn't help me, for I knew and could see people who wanted me jailed. These people needed me out of their way, for nothing other than their own conscience; one Judge said 'this case should have stayed as housekeeping'. He also said 'their libel and slanderous remarks were criminal, and as they were on paper and he had read them they could not be refuted, and he said 'proof of these cruel remarks, are in my transcript'. This time when I stood in the dock, I wasn't alone I had angels standing there with me, invisible but there behind me, in front of me, at my side, I was being protected. My plea was returned to guilty, and the procedure continued.

As I stood in the dock listening as the prosecution read out the evidence compiled about me, such lot of it was hearsay 'not as a rule permissible in a court of law', never mind everyone has their work to do.

The opposition had badgered the police constantly.

I listened to it and then the Judge asked me if there was anything I wanted to say he was looking very hard at me, then sent my lawyer and me out of the room giving me another chance to name anyone else concerned.

I left it as it was, for I was mentally and physically exhausted, 'let's get it over with' I said. I received six months periodic detention, and twelve months supervision. There was nothing else. I wasn't asked for reparation, as the case against me, hadn't been proved; and everything which had been said, was to no avail.

As someone said, I had won my case; I thought and then said 'maybe'? While we were in court and while the Judge was speaking I saw the following.

I kept it to myself for a long time, for no other reason than I didn't think anyone would believe it, and because I wondered if I had really seen it myself, or had it been a figment of my imagination.

I know now it was for real. I have experienced a similar situation, which confirmed my first experience. The Judge was speaking and to my left, his right, I saw a beautiful apparition, I saw beautiful golden flowing robes, I know I stared for a second, and I made a sound, I gasped out loud. The courtroom was dull, the lights were on, but for me it was as if the corner in front of me had brightened up. I thought I was the only one to see this apparition, but I remember the look the Judge gave me, his expression changed for a second, his face went softer.

Anyway as soon as I had seen it, it just rose gently out of sight. In hindsight I know I saw Jesus, and by His presence I knew everything was going to be alright, I am speaking about 'He who repeats a confidence is a fool.' This all happened just after the Judge asked me if there was anyone I would like to name, for he said he didn't believe for one moment I should be the only one standing in the dock, I am not going to say whether this is right or not, I do not have the right to condemn anyone, and it is all history.

History which still rears its ugly head, and may do so always, I have to let it go and move forward.

The Judge's comments and the sentence he passed on me caused a lot of strife, which the media were only too pleased to print. This was done with a pen of cruelty

I read this once, and it suits this situation, 'I was to be misunderstood without explanations' for I have never given any. I was never given the chance. My basic instincts of keeping confidences has been difficult at times, and am very glad I have never broken the rule, the rule I instilled in myself many years ago.

After the court case there was emptiness in me, it had been the only thing to occupy my days for so long; well it seemed to be a long time. What had the suffering been for?

Nothing came out of the court case, nothing had been proven, my saying I was guilty, hadn't been proven either, what had it all been for?

God created me. He chose me. If I emulate Jesus I will suffer as well I am the living evidence we can come through accusations, desertion, rejection and persecution.

We can overcome **everything** when and if we have God's help. My victory was won the day I went down on bended knee, and asked God to come into my heart.

There was an appeal over my sentence, this had to run its course, but when the waiting was over, it was announced the sentence would not be revoked for there wasn't enough evidence, if any at all.

This was to be the end of the matter.

Following this, the media write up printed everything from the start to the finish.

The printing had the right effect to incited readers. The very fact the media printed hearsay, which as I have said is not admissible in a court of law, was in itself evidence they were being fed.

I was given the names of these people, as well as those who wrote asking for the sentence to be revoked.

We have a choice to be ourselves or people pleasers, and we know people pleasers will do what others think is best for them.

They are the ones who go with the flow.

Slanderous letters were written to my publishers who handled my books ordering them not to publish any more of my manuscripts. Beware of what you write and utter.

My heart grieves for not only the accused but also the accuser in anything where persecution is present. Please be aware of what you say especially if your work is in the same field. No one is perfect; if we were **WHY DID JESUS HAVE TO DIE ON THE CROSS?**

There are so many verses in the Bible about tattle telling, and gossip, and each one is delivered with sharpness only God's word has.

There is 'do not speak evil of one another.' Each verse has a warning for us; we must love one another, not some of the time, ALL OF THE TIME. This way we please God and we have a heart which is quiet. I have been through the 'I know best' syndrome and when I did I was expressing doubt to God's word, not a good thing to do, for things will go wrong, they did and I ended up in a mess.

Of course Satan will jump in like a flash and say 'boy you were right to doubt that.' Get out of here Satan, the word is God's and I do believe Him.

Now I listen and try to wait for God, not for Him to catch up as I thought He had to once, but for me to stand still, and wait for His timing.

Many times while I have been writing I have received a rebuke from Him, His voice is as clear as a bell, telling me there is no need for the embroidery, this is when I have rambled on a little.

Well maybe a lot. God's words are very plain, and I have to be plain as well, and by staying plain I do not stray from the facts and the truth. Also I have to be aware facts, are not always, the truth.

Christmas came and went, with my hubby and I sharing Christmas day at Mother's, it was quiet and enjoyable. There was a new learning for each of us for we could not deny the cruelty being dealt to me had shock us. It is sadistic to kick someone when they are down. I have never been able to do this to anyone ever. May God see I never do?

By now I wanted to do nothing else but go back to my home, and after New Year, I did just that, I just packed up, paid my bill and left a part of my life behind in the caravan park.

The hiss of the snake had been taken out beyond the reef; it was time for enmity to be overcome, it was time for self –doubts to disappear, it was time for self to believe in victory, it was time for the calm. It was the time for the walk to and with God to progress. Yes there was a time for everything.


The first few days back in my home found me cleaning and cleaning, there seemed to be something therapeutic in keeping myself busy.

The novelty soon wore off, I must admit and I slowly settled down.

Eventually the day for me to start P.D. arrived and for the next twenty-six weeks I was to have a culture change. This was for real.

Everyone was an offender. Everyone had been branded by man's court of law for some crime or other.

We were all the same no one could feel any different. I won't say I enjoyed it, for some of the work was very difficult, but the wardens well they were the 'wardens', and each person was looked after.

Once I became use to the people and the work, I was able to quietly witness to God, something I did all the time. What I found really difficult to put up with was the blasphemy, I was to cry all the way home one day for swearing seemed to be the only words these people knew.

I prayed about it everyday until I went back the next week, I told the gang I was in I found it offensive. I could have had my teeth pushed down my throat, this didn't happen there was a change though, the swearing didn't actually stop, but if anyone swore near me they would apologise, looking startled as they did so.

Praise the Lord.

There were times while doing P.D. When I was tested beyond what I thought was my endurance, but each day came and went with me having the strength to get to the end.

I feel compassion for young offenders, in any conservative district, and I do not like the attitude many people have towards them. I am not saying I do condone what they have done; I am saying if they are truly repentant, why shouldn't they get another chance. On earth there seems to be an unwritten rule about who is forgiven of their sin and who isn't. Maybe they feel guilty of the sin of omission.

Only the sinless can cast the first stone!

# PART THREE

I had been doing P.D, for a month when our eldest son became ill.

The boy could hardly walk and he looked so grey, I had no idea how serious it was.

He was diagnosed as having a tumour on a kidney. The biopsy confirmed it was cancerous, with him having to have it removed of course. I was now to receive a lesson I will never forget.

I was to learn how to pray, without being selfish.

I prayed and prayed to God not to take my first born son away from me. I begged God to make him better, to leave him alone. I didn't want to lose my son as I had lost my sister, to this painful disease. I had lost so many of my relatives to cancer.

Both of my hubby's parents had succumbed to it, even though there were a few years between their going, it never takes away the fact cancer was the reason for their leaving us.

All of my prayers to God seemed to be of no avail. He was in hospital for most of February and March. I couldn't feel anything other than helplessness. I was trying to come to terms with P.D. and running my home as well.

At no time did I blame anyone for the things which were happening, but I was wondering why God wasn't helping me, He always had before.

Then one day I was to see the light although I wasn't physically hit, I was struck as if by a bolt of lightning. I wasn't praying for my son, I was praying for me. This revelation was so strong I fell on my knees and prayed.

*Dear Father in Heaven, forgive me, I repent for my selfishness, he isn't mine, you lent him to my hubby and I, and he was a precious gift from you to us. I give him back to you Lord; please forgive me for taking so long to see the light.*

*I love you dear Lord, and I live to serve you. Hallelujah.*

When I stood up, it was as if a load had fallen from me, and I could feel my heart quieten. Where I had been begging God to help him, it was with a Mother's agony for my child whom I had carried for nine months. He had been on loan to us, he was a gift, and as soon as I had released him back to God, we were able to go forward.

The sun had started to shine again, metaphorically speaking. I had learnt a very important lesson.

Each time I was taken through another situation I was and am never harmed.

I may think so, but I have always been protected. When I drive along a road, and there is suddenly a dark cloud over me, I do not think as many do, I am under a cloud of doom, I know I am under the wing of God.

He is protecting me for some reason, although I may never know what it is. It makes me feel secure and very positive knowing God loves me so much. The blessings I receive day by day let me know all is well. The world of pain a Mother suffers when faced with the possibility they may lose a child, becomes little less than horrendous, and we lose ourselves in selfish thoughts.

God waits for us to use our situations for His Glory, and then we are able to receive the full love, and help we have prayed for.

If our faith is strong, if we are willing to learn and listen to the Holy Spirit, even if it takes some time, we will always come out being blessed. Remember again God's time is not ours and our day to Him is only a thousand years. God chooses what we endure, this was ordained before we were born, but we choose how we go through it. Godly wisdom we have to learn and I know without God in my life I would be having continuous mishap after mishap. I have to discipline myself to rest in the Lord and wait patiently for Him.

The day I repented to God for being selfish, my son phoned to tell me he was going into hospital to have his operation. I then was to surprise both us, for I said yes I know you are going in next Tuesday, he sounded put out when he said, 'how did you know?' Well how did I know for I certainly hadn't been told? My reply was the Holy Spirit told me. He knew where I was coming from, for I have never made a secret about my commitment to God, if I had it could be misconstrued, and would be almost unforgivable, in my eyes that is. For I am privileged to be a daughter of God!

The operation went without a hitch, and he was able to recover slowly from it, one tumour gone and an oversized kidney less. There is no way it could have been otherwise for we had God on our side.

Although I could write a lot more about him, as I have released him back to God, everything which has followed, are his own experiences. They are his story.

I thank God for letting my hubby and I have the years we had with this delightful child, who is now a man with his own family.

After this and just a few weeks before my P.D. was to end my hubby was to lose his employment.

This was the icing on the cake. Not.

So much had happened to us, all the time we hadn't given a thought to this possibility. It was his work which kept us going, in more ways than one, for it bought in the groceries, and kept up our morale.

## *2Corinthians 12:9 CEV*

**'My kindness is all you need. My power is strongest when you are weak'**

I believe like I believe I have two hands. For God gave me the strength again to walk through my crisis, and as I left everything to Him, we did come out better people.

It was denied, but I believe my court case made us undesirable employees. Some businesses have too many bosses, and this can make for conflicting interests.

Once again there had been a judgement made concerning both of us this time. Nobody will ever know what it did to us. For with the loss of work, we lost our home. The materialistic can be replaced; it was the deceit which went with the situation, my hubby found this most difficult to get over. He put a barrier between himself, and any of the remaining employees and I know he will never trust any of them again. Unless … and this is where God told me to leave well alone.

Nowadays, in the greedy world we live in, the flesh will always put itself first. This is until everyone turns to God for Salvation

### *Proverbs 17:4 CEV*

***Troublemakers listen to troublemakers, and liars listen to liars.***

***Verse 13** **you will always have trouble if you are mean to those who are good to you.***

What a book of wisdom, I love it.

Anyway we lost our work and our home, it was very cruel how it was done, but as I have said I became very strong, and able to stand in the gap, bringing us both through it without too much scathing. God was my helper, He was at my right hand, and He put us where He wanted us to be.

And this was in a lovely cottage, on a farm, where my hubby was able to do some work, and I went forward to receive all the gifts God wanted me to have. The fruit of the Spirit is love, joy peace, kindness, longsuffering, goodness, faithfulness, gentleness and self-control.

### *Galatians 5:22-23 CEV.*

***God's spirit makes us loving, happy, peaceful, patient, kind, good, faithful, gentle, and self controlled. There is no law against behaving in any of these ways.***

### Matthew 6:24 CEV

*You can't be the slave to two masters! You will like one more than the other or be more loyal to one than the other. You can't serve both God and money*

So we either serve our flesh or God. Nobody is excluded are they, for this is what we do? The sins we commit without God are listed for us in Galatians again in ***verses 19-20.CEV***

### Acts 12:2CEV

*The Word of the Lord grew and multiplied*

What happened to me could happen to anyone. The daily paper will tell.

For it all comes down to the fact of people ruling people, where there is persecution of a fellow being. Strangely it has turned out to be my salvation, for I found God. I can hear many saying, Bah!


Unbelievers will, and if they fall into a pit of despair may they turn to God for He is our helper in times of trouble, and He will declare, as He has declared me forgiven, blameless, sinless in His eyes. If you are going through anything distasteful, and unable to see any way out, please do not doubt GOD IS THE ANSWER. It is your choice though, not mine, for you are to make this choice yourself.


The situation we had just gone through brought my hubby and I closer together if it was possible, and I saw him having no difficulty in sitting still, while I read my daily scripture to him and passages from the Bible. He sometimes came in with a remark when I found myself floundering. This happened many times at the beginning of my walk as a Believer. I would be asked a question and if I didn't have the answer on my heart regarding it, I went to my Bible for answers; I didn't always find a solution. Further along the road in God's time, in God's way, the question may have been answered but once again in His timing.

I have noticed I am great on timing, and it is very important to take note God's time is not necessarily ours.

**You can not teach what you do not know; and you can not lead where you have not been.**

I read this somewhere, and I find it very helpful to remember.

Going to Christian meetings was a problem, and it shouldn't have been, I believed Christians would not judge anyone; they are not our judge, sadly though they do judge.

Many looked at me and went as far as asking me why I was there. It seemed beyond their comprehension for me to be at a Christian meeting after being labelled; they didn't believe I had the right, and went as far as telling me so.

These Christians labelled me as undesirable; please remember Saint Paul murdered Jews, before God got a hold of him. He actually did murder them. Through the attitude of these worldly Christians, I develop an attitude of unworthiness.

Attitudes can change day by day; also attitudes can be what we base our daily decisions on. I came through this, for God continued to educate me, and although I still get an attitude and who doesn't, it is our reaction to it that God watches. I know God; and through my knowledge of Him I am able to stay balanced in my actions. And yes I do go off the rails, now and again.

As I said it when I was reading the Bible to my hubby, from the book of Timothy I suddenly realised he believed God was looking out for us both as well as me. This was a great comfort to me for the Bible says in

*Matthew 18:19-20 CEV, whenever two or three come together in my name I am there with you.*

We moved from one house to another with the intention of starting a new life. There was no sadness with moving at all, for both of us needed to have a fresh start, a new life and this was the way for us to achieve it.

We both wanted to have a new beginning with only daily ups and downs. Jesus has not promised Christians a cushy life. If we are comfortable, we may not be doing what we should be, spreading the 'Word of God'. It would be lovely if every heart I touch with my story was a heart ready to receive salvation through Christ Jesus, and the love of the Father in Heaven the Father, who created us.

Our moving went smoothly enough, I had no idea where everything was going to fit, we put furniture, books anything which was not wanted for our immediate use in a spare room, the only spare room, for this cottage only had two bedrooms, large living area, and the necessary rooms, kitchen etc. The washhouse had a shower in it, a bathroom and the smallest room lived up to being just about the smallest room I have ever seen. These entire things aside, it was a beautiful cottage to live in, and as we had God with us, there was a peace which embraced you each time you entered.

I am a real woman, one who likes a change every now and then, so we have the furniture moved about, this can add spice to ones life, especially if one changes it back to the former position the next day, as I have done.

There was a little happening, when we went to get the last load of furniture, My hubby and I went off not really enjoying ourselves but we had to do this last gathering of our belongings. While I was digging plants out, a feeling of doubt overcame me.

Had we done the right thing choosing this place, if it wasn't I suppose I could pass the buck, and say it was my hubby's choice?

This would have been wrong of course, for the final choice we made together, but really it was God who led us to it. Maybe we could blame Him if things went wrong. This never entered my head to do so as the plan was there, we made the choice to move, and anyway where else could we go.

Negative thoughts raced through my head, all from the darkness of Satan, who tried his best to unsettle me.

This wasn't healthy, and I immediately started to pray, and did I pray, 'Please God, show me it is right, forgive me for having these doubts.' I went on while I was digging, although I was still uncertain in my head, my heart only felt peace.

At last, the load was ready for the trip to our new home, and we set off. As we were approaching our new home, I looked up and there was a rainbow, this was strange for the day wasn't overcast it was fine, but there was the rainbow, we both saw it, and yes it was over the new house.

**PRAISE THE LORD. HALLELUJAH.**

*Judges 6:36-37 CEV Gideon prayed to God,' I know that you promised to help me rescue Israel, but I need proof. Tonight I'll put some wool on the stone floor of that threshing-place over there. If you will really help me rescue Israel, then tomorrow morning let there be dew on the wool, but let the stone floor be dry.*

It is permitted to put out a fleece to God, to test, everything had gone so smoothly in getting this house, we wanted to be sure we got it through the right channels, we had so many ups and downs served us, we just had to be sure. I asked for a visual sign. God who knows me and knows I believe the rainbow is a promise from Him. So there you have it. Hallelujah.

It took my hubby and me some time to get use to the life of the semi retired. There seem to be very little to do, I put the house into shape, and made some easy care gardens, then what was I to do?

I started to get lonely, I didn't know anyone here, the truth of the matter was I didn't trust anyone enough to visit them to say hello.

The months went by; I was in constant touch with my friend talking over the phone most days, she was the only Christian I was in contact with.

I went out and did housework for some people, not enjoying it at all, but we needed the money I earned.

I was able to do some knitting for others, but this was something although I liked doing it, I had said after my last book was published, I wouldn't get involved with anyone through my crafts. I started to have self –doubts again; I felt maybe I wasn't meant to live here; and I it was like this until a year later when, I realised God had me here for a reason.

## *Isaiah 40: 31 CEV*

*But those who trust the Lord will find new strength. They will be strong like eagles soaring upwards on wings; they will walk and run without getting tired*

I was resting, in this lovely place of peace, and when God was ready for me to go out into the world I would do so with a Godly outlook on everything.

Isn't God beautiful?

I spent time recovering from everything which had gone before, I learnt to lean upon the 'Word of God', from the Bible, and I learnt to pray and to trust God more. I was able to do these things because I had no distractions.

I was also to learn God **does** know what He is doing, His ways are not our ways, and His time is not our time his ways are higher than ours. I know I keep on about God's timing but it is so important to understand our Christian walk is in God's timing, and everything we do always!

## *Psalms 37:7 CEV*

*Be patient and trust the Lord.*

I have written that quotation on a stone, which is there for all to see it, at my back door.

I started going to prayer meetings for fellowship, I will not say I enjoyed them, but it was a start.

I heard every time, how someone had been a Christian for so many years, and I felt out of my depth.

As a new Christian I found the confidence of other Christians intimidating feeling anything I contributed in prayer and praise too feeble, and I felt it was better to stay silent, I was to discover it is alright to be silent to listen and learn.

One day I went to hear a speaker, it said on the invitation 'a gifted Christian Evangelist, with a ministry in healing'. Also on the invite were the words,

**_Revelations 3:20 CEV_**

**_Listen I am standing and knocking at your door._**

I went with three others, arriving early.

The first people I saw were three women who were some of the accusers involved with my court case.

This threw me a little, strangely enough I never thought to pray but I wasn't really worried, God had me at this place and His Glory would be in it somewhere. One of these ladies came over to me and asked me who I was? When I told her, she gave me a big hug. Saying she was sorry for the episode I had just been through.

I was completely dumbfounded for this was a new experience. I usually have a few (ha, ha) intelligent remarks for most situations. This time no go. This lady was really sorry she was genuine.

Believe me readers sometimes 'hugs and words' can be so cheap, done for the wrong reasons. It is done to appease yourself, or for people to see you. But this was neither of those, it was genuine. The hug was forgiveness, her to me, and me to her. It had to happen for both of us to move forward

Remember always follow forgiveness with forgiving actions.

The day went on and I found I was at peace; I also found the ladies in question didn't bother me. Although I was aware they were there, as they were with me no doubt.

In the afternoon sitting listening to the guest speaker, she said there has been a healing, and I heard someone near me say 'I know'.

And so we came to the end of the days meeting. And back home again I told my hubby when he came in, all about it, end of subject.

After I said my prayers the next morning instead of my usual shower I had a bath.

As the water flowed away I realised something was different there seemed to be 'No what next' feelings within me, yes I suddenly realised I was healed from all my hurt completely, I had been cleansed naturally and when I told a friend she said, 'I know and I know when you received the healing'. Yes, it was at the meeting the day before when the speaker said 'there has been a healing'.

My body had been spiritually cleansed. Praise the Lord. He had been tenderly looking out for me until I was ready to receive it, He had me at the meeting for His purpose. When we feel, as if He is nowhere near us we are to remember, He will never leave, or forsake you, He has said this.

The Lord's Prayer says 'on earth as it is in Heaven' what has happened in heaven [spiritually] should happen on earth [naturally]. This is the same as 'From God's mouth to my ear, and from my mouth to God's ear' what I pray before delivering a message in church.


Before I was filled with the Holy Spirit there were many occasions when I took upon myself the burden of actions and spoken words, of what another had said and done. Even though I knew this was wrong I would still do it.

Now as a Christian I carry the truth within me, I am not responsible for anything other than what I do or say myself. Even if it is gossip or written about me, if I didn't write it or say it, it is not my problem, and this goes for you as well. We are not responsible for another's actions or words.

If you have done or said something wrong go to God, and ask for forgiveness take accountability of the wrong, acknowledge the fact you did it, and for what purpose.

This is a certainty; we must repent of our own actions and words, we will always have an issue for cleansing to be the person God wants us to be. If you are an unbeliever you will still have to make amends somehow, for you will never be comfortable with the people you injured.

If you want a clean and healthy life, and want to live without your wrong actions hanging over you, the choice of doing right or wrong is yours.

We have always had this choice; everything we do will revolve around it. Choice is an axel for right and wrong just as we have the tree of knowledge of good and bad.

When I was first saved or 'born again', I listened and understood many Christians, at the same time though I was to misunderstand many, I wasn't confident enough to go to my Bible for confirmation on what I had heard. I believed them; in fact I stood in awe of them, they had known the Lord for many years longer than I had, well they said so as if it was a crime not to be where they were. I was looking at people not God and through this I became confused.

I started to doubt myself, not God; it was these doubts which played havoc with my emotions. They led me to believe my feelings, not the truth; I am speaking about God's truth, not man's, for we know man can change day to day, depending on the situation. The truth of God never changes.

Then I was to reason with myself, I was to hinder God, to reason is a natural thing, and God is, supernatural.

### *Colossians 3:1-2 CEV*

***You have been raised to life with Christ. Now set your heart on what is in heaven, where Christ rules at God's right side. Think about what is up there, not about what is here on earth***

We must learn to pray in every situation giving our requests to God, not man he can do nothing spiritually. We learn to seek comfort from the Holy Spirit.

## *Matthew 6:25 CEV*

### *I tell you not to worry about your life*

With my doubts, I started to feel guilty; everyone will have had this guilt trip at some time or other, and through my lack of self worth, self esteem, I thought I wasn't good enough for God, thinking I should know Him and all his teachings in the twinkling of an eye.

A lifetime isn't long enough to learn the wonders of Him, he is patient, he is kind and when we repent we are forgiven and his grace is towards us.

We must not let Satan confuse us. He is the master of deception.

## *Ephesians 4:27CEV*

### *Don't give the devil a chance.* (Give no opportunity to him)

It is our faith which gives us access to God, and we can listen to our hearts where He dwells. When His heart lines up with His word and the quickening of the Holy Spirit we have the true witness of what God speaks.

By having faith in God, and believing in Him, we can tell this mountain (our guilt) to be removed and be cast into the sea.

## *Mark 11:23CEV*

### *If you have faith in God and don't doubt, you can tell this mountain to get up and jump into the sea, and it will.*

This peace is beyond understanding, and it will guard your heart, (Spirit) and mind (Soul) in Christ Jesus.

Truth is a person. He is Jesus, for He said, *'I am the truth, I can set you free'.* It is through God's guidance and His truth I have become totally, totally free, I am now a free spirit with God. It is through this freedom I can write knowing it is the truth. I am writing God's words to you my reader; God is speaking to you through me. God is with me as I am writing, looking out for me and you. Also He is giving me added strength for any Godly walk I may have in the future. I am not able to be God, but I emulate

Jesus, so my walk must be holy and how I see the world Godly. I know whatever I am asked to do, I will be able to endure it, for hasn't He said He will not take us beyond our endurance? He will show me what He wants me to do, at the right time. He knows I understand I have a choice, whether I do it, or not. I know if I don't do it, I will not receive the blessing. I also know if I don't do it He will call someone else to do so. There is little to worry here though for everything I do, is for the Glory of God. Praise the Lord. Hallelujah.

Truth is the 'Word of God'.

So seek ye the truth.

Do not listen to mans interpretation of God's Word, unless you know He is totally committed to serving the one who created him, or your walk may be brought into confusion, and confusion as I have said is not of God. Please God may my readers be released through the revelation of the truth from the scriptures about any doubts in their heart on living both in the natural world and the Spiritual realm.

*Therefore if anyone is in Christ, he is a new creation; old things have passed away; behold, all things have become new.*

In *Galatians*, we are told we have been redeemed, from the curse of the law. We receive the promise of the Spirit through our faith. As believers we are under the covering of God where He wants us.

God spoke all these words

**Exodus 20:1 CEV**

*God said to the people of Israel 'I am the Lord your God...'*

*BUT I SHOW LOVE TO THOUSANDS OF GENERATIONS OF THOSE WHO LOVE ME, AND OBEY MY LAWS*

There is no argument is there? For God Himself spoke those words. This is the end of it. Because I love God, I trust Him, because I love God I can fear Him, do not be confused, if we fear God we have no need to fear man, nobody can stand against Him, I believe Him and I obey Him, I am under His covering. I do not have to carry guilt for what another has done. Listen here anything I have taken on board, whether I have heard it, or maybe someone has told me 'you are etc', not realising I had taken into my heart the comments. I must rebuke the words and cast them away from me in the name of Jesus. We sometimes take into our hearts what seemingly could be just everyday things. But God tells us what to take on, and when to leave well alone. If we listen again to this scripture

## *Luke 10: 19 CEV*

*I have given you the power to stand on snakes and scorpions and to defeat the power of your enemy Satan. Nothing can harm you*

## *Proverbs 3:5-6CEV*

*With all your heart, you must trust the Lord, and not on your own judgement. Always let him lead you and he will clear the road for you to follow.*

If someone thinks you have a problem with you life, (your character) and you are quoted a verse from the Bible, over this problem, do not take it on board, (into your heart), take it to your Bible, read it, verses above and below, no go, you don't feel anything - meditate on Gods word – wait He will give you understanding. Sometimes the understanding can be in two parts.

Just go to God, pray it out, He will show you, He will listen, He will answer. You may find one day someone in a ordinary conversation may throw light on a previously unanswered question, they may well be oblivious to the light you have received, you may to at the time, but the revelation will come later for the word of God will have gone to your heart, where he resides.

Who are we to tell someone else about their character?

I often get the answer from hearing the word being preached; sometimes I have received it by sharing with a Christian friend. I seek always the three witnesses. As I have said our hearts must line up with God's word.

A child of God is protected through the name and blood of Jesus.

The door of my home is always open to those who come in peace. I have sealed the doors from evil, and windows the high ways and the low ways, meaning the power lines and the underground water ways into the house, through prayer with the blood of Jesus, and I have no doubt in my heart nothing or nobody will ever enter, if they have evil intent. The household is protected through the blood of Jesus entirely.

I had many ornaments in my home and I was told they were of occult origin, they may well have been, but as a craft person although I might have known what they were I only saw the promise of a project in them.

Because they were offensive to others they have been removed, their removable was another dimension. For I was told they were representing, occult activity which came from my ancestors.

I am not under any ancestral curses. If I had been they went to the Cross with Jesus, when I went to the Cross physically and fell down on my knees in humble awe, repenting of all my own, and family sins, and all the curses I had taken upon myself.

Having these things in my home, was my ignorance of God's truth, which made me believe I was being sinful.

We have also Christian counsel. I do not always get the answer I am expecting, but the answer I always get is God inspired. Hallelujah.

I have had the choice to be positive or negative; when I wake up in the morning I have my first choice of the day, to be happy or unhappy.

As I go through my day I may sin, not because I want to but I may, either by words or actions, but I will never stop believing Jesus rose again from the dead, our improper thoughts can be our downfall. I may sometimes think something which to an unbeliever is nothing; in fact it may appear to be a very ordinary thought. I may point a finger at someone, which would be critical, and I may trip over my feet going out the door, and blaspheme. These are sins in God's eyes.

In God's eyes these sins are the same as planning a murder, pointing a gun at someone and pulling the trigger, they are no different. If we do lie a small white lie; to God it is a sin. **It is a big sin.**

*Isaiah 59:1CEV The Lord hasn't lost his powerful strength; he can still hear and answer prayers.*

*Verse 12 How often have we sinned and turned against you, the Lord God?*
*Our sins condemn us! We have done wrong.*

**Isaiah 58:9 CEV**

*When you beg the Lord for help, he will answer 'Here I Am.'*

I had to learn all the things God sees as sin. We have already talked about them. I had to learn the differences between saying sorry, and repentance. Saying sorry can be like saying hello, when I don't hear something I will say 'sorry'. But being sorry to the Lord must be like the verse from

**_Psalms 38:18 CEV_**

*I told you about my sins and I am sorry for them.*

Any sin I take upon myself I am answerable for, no one else. I repeat once again. Repent means more than saying sorry; more even than to change ones mind. It involves a complete turn around from independence of God, to dependence on Him.

When I sin, I feel cold, I can feel the grief of our Lord, I know He grieves for me.

## *Psalm 23:1CEV*

### *You Lord are my shepherd; I will never be in need.*

There are many verses through the Psalms which describe how I feel when I go astray, the hatred, and revenge I felt when I went through the court case, the rejection I have put on others by not seeing they needed my forgiveness, these are all sins I had to repent from.

I am not going to say letting anyone who has hurt you know they have your forgiveness it is not that easy to do, but it is right and proper for you to do so. I can ask for the wisdom for the days ahead for I do not like being negative. You see I have the choice again, but I opt for the positive, God lets me choose, if I sin in any way and He knows I have repented He will strengthen me.

## *Isaiah 44:22CEV*

### *Turn back to me I have rescued you, and swept away your sins as though they were clouds* DON'T YOU LOVE THAT?

And I am not going to say we must get down on our knees to ask repentance, God hears us wherever we call from, and there are some who can express themselves better on our knees. I myself go to my knees when I am able to and especially when my heart is so full, I believe situations can knock us to our knees, and of course we then are in the perfect position to pray, aren't we? I give thanks to the Lord, for each day, and I ask for his wisdom, to help me keep my mouth closed when it should be, and to speak when I the time is right

**Ecclesiastes,3 CEV** *there is a time for everything'*; I love this book, and always end up laughing when I read it.

### *3:1*

*Everything on earth has its own time and its own season.* The triple test is there as well

*5:2-6 Don't talk before you think or make promises to God without thinking them through. God is in heaven and you are on earth, so don't talk too much. If you keep thinking about something, you will dream about it. If you talk too much, you will say the wrong thing. God doesn't like fools. So don't be slow to keep your promises to God. It is better not to*

***make a promise at all than to make one and not keep it. Don't let your mouth get you in trouble. And don't say to the worship leader 'I didn't mean what I said' God can destroy everything you have worked for, so don't say something that makes God angry.***

***Is it true***, to say something, ***is it kind*** to say something, and ***is it necessary*** to repeat something? Sometimes it is all three. We have only to look through our Bible for God's words, and by following the laws within the covers, we can grow spiritually.

Anyone can read the Bible from cover to cover, I have never done this myself, I have read and read a part I like, and even been able to recite verses from the same chapter, but this is not what the Bible is about.

If we are making something, we follow instructions don't we? Well this is what the Bible is. A book of instructions, it is full of God's instructions, for our daily living.

Christians to receive the everlasting benefits from the living word (our Bible) we must learn and understand what God has written for us. As God dwells in our hearts, we not only need to read these words, we must obey them, and this is if we want to survive in the human world. Once we become Christians we are responsible for the sharing of God's word, and we must do this in the love we are privileged to have received from Him. We share the word in faithful service to a God we can call our heavenly Father. Hallelujah.

To share words in love we will have listeners, but be careful for I was to run amok here.

I was very timid when I first became a Christian, and found it was easier to read than to speak out. Then I was to make a mistake, one I can say I am thankful for, as I have learnt from it. I became very devout, or another word religious – walking in the flesh not the spirit, I was to pass on messages although they were Bible based, Satan used me. I had a religious spirit. I was blind to this though. I was to say, 'the Lord says' over and over again. Whenever I opened my mouth out would pop something the Lord had said. If your gifts are ministry and you want to speak to someone, seek God most earnestly before speaking into someone's life. If you are on the right track they themselves will have been given some word of recognition to what you are saying.

You may make or break them. The wrong words are cheap. The person you passed the so-called message on to may have said you have been forgiven, but you may find the forgivers actions don't line up with the words. You ask forgiveness, how the other person reacts is not your problem it's between them and God. I know what gossip can be. I know also what harm it can do. All through my court case, not one person came to me and asked what was going on, they were happy enough to spread malicious rumour, gossip, and hearsay, whispering, behind my back, reporting comments they had heard. Before you utter before God, you must have heard with your own ears, seen with your own eyes. Otherwise it is gossip. If doubtful, don't, speak against anyone, if you can find no words of kindness about a person, keep your mouth shut, and take it to God.

He, who doubts is condemned - whatever is not from faith, is sin.


### *Romans 14: 22 CEV*

*What you believe about these things should be kept between you and God. You are fortunate, if your actions don't make you have doubts.*

As I advanced through my Christian walk many spoke into my life.

I was to get over the hurt I had taken on board through ignorance. I have forgiven those whom I felt could have told me with more sensitivity about my failings.

'He who casts the first stone'.


I was still to look for a place of God where I would be just another free Christian, and I found it by going to a Bible school. This is really a joke for I am not a student, God must have thought, I needed a lesson. I was to go to this school, and slowly I was to come out of the many things which hindered me. I had to give my testimony in two minutes, it actually took five minutes, I had to stand up in front of the class, and I had to tell them how I became a Christian myself.

I enjoy writing and I used to enjoy speaking in public, but I lost my confidence. I said I would never stand up in front of a crowd of people again. God had other ideas on this matter. I was to stand up twice to speak while going to this school, and do you know both times I enjoyed it.

Well when they were over, I realised I had enjoyed them.

Once many years before I became a Believing Believer there was a time when I went to a Pentecostal church and when I went in everyone was waving their arms in the air, and falling all over the place, I thought I was the only sane person there, but this was my ignorance, for I had no idea what it was all about. I join in and I myself became a wave my arms person in praise to God, and I fell over as well. When the Holy Spirit touched me big time I had no idea what I was going to do, I will tell you each time I was touched I want more. It was between God and me. One of the things I was to pray about with regularity was 'why am I unable to speak in strange tongues'. Well the Bible says we may do.

When I became a Spirit filled Christian I didn't speak in tongues until about four years later. One morning after I had asked God to help me through a situation, and to forgive me for my attitude, an attitude I did not own, so I thought, it was someone else's, (ha), it wasn't. After I had asked God to forgive me for this, I suddenly started to speak in tongues.

I was excited, I hadn't a clue what I was saying, and couldn't wait for my hubby to hear me, and when eventually he did, I can still see his face and hear him say, 'don't let the neighbours hear you'.

Speaking in tongues is between the speaker and God, unless someone interprets it, nobody can understand what you say. It is your own heavenly language and the thing I found wonderful was, Satan is unable to understand it either.

Speaking in tongues is a gift from the Holy Spirit,

## *1Corinthians 12: 8-10* *CEV*

I am like Paul, for when I was unable to speak in tongues myself I would think I was out on a limb. I wasn't confused, but I wished I had this same gift so I could pray to God expressing the depth of my love for I could never find the right words in my natural tongue.

There are times when something happens in my life and I go to God in prayer about it, as I pray in my natural tongue, I feel as if I am not giving God my all, I am also having to think about the words I am putting together, for this is how my brain works, then I became choked up. Suddenly my head becomes controlled by my heart, the Holy Spirit takes over and away I go into tongues. Then I receive a peace and slowly my body is no longer in torment, I am able to see what I have to do to resolve my problem. God shows me.

**That is beautiful**,

Hang in here with me for a minute, remember I wasn't able to speak this heavenly language for four years, and God and I still managed to overcome difficult situations, well God did. The timing once again was God's not mine. He gave me the gift of tongues, not when I wanted it, when He knew I would be able to use it for His glory. He loosed my tongue, so these strange words could drip off it like honey. God, Jesus who is The Word, the Holy Spirit, (three in one) it is they who understand what I am praying. They answer me, of this I know. If you haven't the gift of tongues, please do not feel you have been forgotten; I put myself through many senseless questions before my tongue was released.

We are all given what God knows we need. Not what we ourselves want. At the end of the day I find every one of my daily needs have been met. Praise the Lord, O how I love Him. So you see it's in the speaking of tongues although it is beautiful, it is personal, something even more beautiful is God's love which he covers every Christian with. And longs for the unsaved –

## *John 12:47CEV*

*I am not the one who will judge those who refuse to obey my teachings. I came to save the people of this world, not to be their judge*

Do not get me wrong here every one who is a Christian, will go down the path of growth as I have. There is no easy way to learn God's ways; and nobody knows His plans for us. His ways are not our ways. I have said this time and time again

We are not condemned for our natural feelings, but we must be careful what we do with them. God will use our pain; of this we can be sure. God has used the pain I went through to help me in my new life with Him, for I am his servant, and I go forward, He never promised me an easy life as a Christian, when it becomes too easy I wonder where have I missed the path, what have I missed out? We must not let the situation or the circumstances around control us; we must exercise our faith, to overcome them. We are not to be anxious about anything, we must always pray, this way we will always be the winner.

The pain I was to suffer made me sensitive to others, God uses this and I have many times been quickened to see the same pain in someone else. I am filled with compassion, something I may well have in the past, but not with the insight I now have. I have been given the gift of a very powerful discerning spirit. I am not boasting it is the plain truth. By using this gift as God meant it to be, I have been able to help many people who were put in my face so to speak. I can still help someone, somewhere, and I know it is the Word of God working through me.

I have no idea who is going to read this but I do know there are many who will be able to get help from it if they do.

### *2 Corinthians 5:1CEV*

*Our bodies are like tents that we live in here on earth. But when these tents are destroyed, we know that God will give each of us a place to live.*

The next part of my story will show you how God is working through my life for there is no way any of it would have come into being without Him. I was glancing through some papers one day when I spotted this advertisement.

A bus company wanted a school bus driver, I read it, thinking I would love to be with children for I had always involved myself with them, but had back stepped, thinking it wouldn't be appropriate because of my past. I put the thought away, and went outside to have a drink in the sun. I do not know how this happened, for I only remember taking out my chair and cup, but the paper came too, opened at the advert. I read it again with a feeling of excitement, and then put it out of my mind, but for the next two hours everywhere I went so did the paper. Suddenly I decided to ring up the company and ask for an interview.

I am telling you here I didn't have the necessary qualifications to get this position. When I rang I was asked if I would like to have an interview, and I said yes. This was starting to get out of hand, well I thought so anyway. The interview was different, I had never been in this situation before, usually it was me doing the interviewing, anyway I told everything I needed to including I had a record, nobody battered an eyelid, then I told them I didn't have the appropriate driver's license, once again nobody choked at my nerve. I was told to go to the police station and apply for it.

And again, I was to enter into a world I had declared I would never enter again.

I applied for a licence stating of course about the criminal record and paid up for what is the normal procedure to begin. This procedure went on for some time; I was interviewed by the Lands and Transport Department.

This was in my home and once again I had to go over the court case. This wasn't easy, but I managed to get through it. It is not a subject I mention but I am able to now, for it did happen, and there is no running away from it, at the time of the interview it was difficult still very fresh in my mind.

Everything about getting my license has been God ordained, for in the natural I would never have tried for it.

The court case was looked into and came and went, nothing there to stop the procedure. It was as if my past hadn't happened.

Then my health had to be given the third degree, if it hadn't been I would have doubted the department a little. For driving a bus is a big responsibility, there are people in your care. I am glad my health was thoroughly scrutinised.

Here is something, which makes me feel very humble.

After my first interview I was given the job, subject to getting the license.

I had a driving instructor, who taught me the ins and outs of driving a bus, when the first lesson was over I felt as if my shoulders would never be the same. I am not a very tall person, and everything seemed to be so big.

I wasn't put off though, I was happy. My health passed the test, and I was granted permission to sit the license.

Just because I had been driving a car for many, many years, didn't automatically make me a good driver, actually there had been times when going to town I wondered how I got there. Obviously no such chances can be taken with transporting the public, especially children you must be 100% alert.

I was to get my license passing the questions which are on a scratchy 25 out of 25, and the oral questions; I passed 9 and a half out of 10. When it came to the practical I passed also. Praise the Lord. Driving is no trouble to me I enjoy it, there is a twist here now though, for I do not get into the driver's seat of our car as much as I use to.

Through God's grace, I became a qualified bus driver, and I loved it.

When I first looked at this work I thought it was a voluntary job, so once again I was to receive God's grace, for I found each week I received a pay packet. Praise the Lord. When we do something which is out of the ordinary, we can expect the hand of God has been guiding us along. Hallelujah.

*Have you ever driven a school bus?*

*I have and do!*

*It is full of laughing children*

*For that is what they do.*

*Some think they are smart,*

*Some are gentle and kind*

*But there is one thing I can tell you*

*They are all little loves of mine.*


### '*Bring the little children unto me*' said Jesus.

And this is what I was doing while driving my bus.

I now walk along a path with flowers each side of it, they are peace, love, serenity, pleasure, comfort, ease, gratification and contentedness, they grow each day within me through the daily word I read, I have become a free spirit; I can live each day praising God for the love, and grace and mercy He bestows upon me. Even though I still felt, I hadn't reached the ultimate.

I would sometimes wonder what I was missing, but there didn't seem to be anything.

It is God's timing again, for He put someone of whom I barely knew in my path. It was while we were talking I was asked if I would like to be water baptised, and suddenly everything became bright, and I said "yes please". I was so excited for I knew God wanted me to be water baptised in obedience to the command of our Lord Jesus Christ and in imitation of his very own example.

I have a printed certificate saying I am living by faith in the Son of God, who loved me and gave Himself for me

When I was baptised I felt very lonely, for there was nobody of my own with me. I thought about this, I don't believe Jesus had anyone with him either really that day when he was also in the Jordan river baptised, I was in a room full of Christians, but they were all strangers, and they really didn't want to speak to me, yes I did feel lonely. I must look at that again, I had a barrier around me maybe there were some there who did want to speak I didn't let them.

As I came up out of the water I heard 'This is my daughter, and I am well pleased with her, she is my treasure.' And from that very moment I have never been bothered about being on my own, for everyone who is a Believing Believer is my family and God is my Father. Whether they speak to me or not. Praise the Lord for the revelation.

It was four years after becoming a Believing Believer; I was to reach my ultimate, through my obedience to God. And become as we are commanded water baptised

I love my life. Each day is different, there are times when I would like the day to hurry up and end. Only because I wouldn't slow down, and there are those days I wish would never end.

I have enjoyed some Christian camps. They confirmed for me there is something at camps for you whatever and wherever you are with God.

For my first camp I travelled with two women, I wasn't really sure what I was letting myself into. I had no idea what was going to happen. My thoughts wandered as we travelled and at times I joined in the conversation. Would I know anyone? Who was going to be there? Silly things went through my head, I was stepping out of my comfort zone, and when we do this it is a little scary.

We travelled for an hour, before we arrived, and then name tags, along with the room allocation. 'Oh dear', I wouldn't know my room companions; it didn't really cause any issues, there was acceptance, and why not for we were all sisters in Christ? Weren't we?

God taught me a good lesson about Christian camps; do not look for what's not there, but take what is there.

There was the first meal, this was different, nobody jumped the queue and nobody pushed, there was laughing and quiet talking, while each waited their turn.

The camp was opened, and the first meeting was to begin, this was when the Holy Spirit came upon us, and took over, when dedicated Christians are in a room it is like an electric current running through each one, linking them together, and believe me this is what happened. The guest speakers were under the powerful anointing of God.

You could feel the power of the Holy Spirit in every corner of the room, and if you didn't it was because you were not receptive to it. I was to sway backwards, forwards and sideways on my feet, glad there was a chair in front of me to hold on to. I love the power of the Holy Spirit filling me. And although I carry the Holy Spirit with me all the time as anyone will do if they are walking closely to God, I have learnt to retain it within myself, I breathe deeply and let it saturated me when the anointing arises it is then I may receive a word of wisdom either to deliver or as a warning for my protection. I allow God, to give me all I need through His grace.

When I arrived I was thinking 'now I am here I might as well make the most of it', and it wasn't very long before I said, "I want this weekend to go on forever".

When you open your heart to the Holy Spirit this is what can happen. It is freedom and those who wanted to laugh, shout, stamp their feet were able to do so through God's grace and nobody noticed for they were also the same.

We often feel we don't want to look foolish, let me tell you, nobody sees you as the person who came to the meeting they see you as God sees you; they see the love of God shining in, and through you.

I must say, I am unable to answer for anyone else, only myself. and this is what I see, as a Spirit filled Christian I pray this is what everyone will see as well.

I accepted the gift of discernment from God after a battle, for I didn't at the time feel I needed to know what He revealed to me, now I thank Him daily for it as I am able to encourage, and to share His love to others. Yes I am thankful for I have been given a double portion to help others; I have accepted Gods' purpose in my life.

### *Hebrews 5:14 CEV*

**Solid food is for mature people who have been trained to know right from wrong.**

*A discerning Spirit sees with the eye of understanding*

*A discerning Spirit sees the truth*

*A discerning Spirit can discern both good and evil*

God will fill me with such compassion sometimes for another, and this is beautiful, for in the flesh I mightn't go anywhere near the needy person. I want to tell you I have had all the rigid rules removed from me, the rules which say, you must never shout, you must never make a spectacle of yourself, you must never do this, you must never do that, these are the rules of man, not Gods'.

These are the rules which restrain us from freedom, they are our inhibitions and I have finally managed to get rid of them. This has made me completely blind to the criticism which comes from an unbeliever. God has control of me, and He will never let me be embarrassed by my actions. Well He is a gentleman and wouldn't would He?

The most important thing God has removed is the obstruction from my ears it was a stumbling block, and I can now hear what I say. So when I say, I would enjoy doing this I now hear me saying it, and find I take it on board to do what I have to do when the situation arises. I know I have to hear what He and I say for I am told to listen, and heed.

If you love God your creator, and if you serve him daily, you will live a full life of contentment. You will be happy with what you have. You will always be safe. You will never be lonely, for you will always have someone with you, who will be your friend and guide you.

Someone to guide you along a path which is narrow, but full of beauty.

There are two people who will always love you, the ***most important one*** is ***GOD***, and the other one is me. ***HALLELUJAH***

# THE CONCLUSION

**In these final pages we have the closing of a door, and a summary of my understanding to all I have written. Most importantly is my tribute to my hubby.**

I pour out my deep understanding to widows and widowers. One has to experience the loosing of a life's partner to know the grief it brings.

Daily thought changes do not lessen the pain which sometimes is intensified, and as we learn to live without the one we chose to be our loving husband or wife in the presence of God, we will survive for we have the hand of strength to hold and lead us, for we are over comers. We are to hold on to our memories and be grateful, we have them.

There have been many comments about my story as I have talked it over with other writers, and I didn't expect otherwise, it hasn't been written for anyone to avenge themselves through this reading, it is an instrument of love to my neighbour, a love you are to pick up and pass to yours. And if you are reading this there certainly is something between the covers for you.

Through the intervening years of experience there have been many changes in the family, and I have been given the privilege to put them on paper. My mother's heart was pulled in five different directions at times and all from love for my children and husband.

The wandering feet, and deceitful heart in the beginning, have been planted firmly on the rock of salvation, making sure I never falter and I stay inclined toward the love and strength of the one who called me.

Yes, He called me, and like Samuel I replied 'here I am' giving the gentle King permission to live within my heart.

The love of God will always guide my fingertips, over the keyboard through His residency within me, what ever story I am writing.

The past events can never change, and it is not advisable for anyone to believe looking back and keeping attitudes of the past will be of benefit, this is not so if they want to walk in the **Shekinah Glory of God.**

## *If <u>you take</u> what <u>you want</u> God says, '<u>you will have to pay for it</u>'.*

The past is nothing other than history.

At the end of each day history is made; the future is in going forward.

There are moments of remembrance when past issues bring sadness, and hang heavily over us.

The answer is we are to deal with all past issues, so the heart can stay clean and stable, in a love only the Saviour of our soul can bring.

When there is disharmony within a family accountability, of both actions and words must happen for a healing to be complete.

This goes for the disharmony in the world as well; the guilty must repent to be acceptable to the real and true master of life. Satan who uses people to do his dirty work can do nothing without the permission of God. When we dither on the edge of doubt with hums and ahs, we are only leaving a door open for him to enter into our lives.

## *Hebrews 11:3CEV*

*Because of our faith, we know that the world was made at Gods command. We also know that what can be seen was made out of what can't be seen.*

Unless our faith is strong and our life is in the Master's hands, we do not see the devil in people it becomes obvious when one tries to master the other. We know God's children by their fruits, we are encouragers, and will never discourage a sister or brother in Christ.

The serpents head has to be crushed to quell his hissing.

My knowledge of the Lord Jesus, has taught me doom and gloom will smother the Believing Believer in a moment if there is just one small gap of vulnerability, and my relationship which has strengthened and led me into eternal protection through the blood and name of Jesus, has a fight on its hands, my faith, my belief will not allow any demons to trespass. Negativity is negative!

In every single conscious moment of my life I am to be alert, and keep myself from thoughts of doubt.

To explain this last sentence I am told to be alert of the roaring lion out there waiting to devour me, which means I must be aware of temptation, and not fall into the trap of self pity, or any other negative action, I must allow the Holy Spirit control in leading me through green pastures beside the quiet waters.

As many understandings come from what has just been written, I listen to the Spirit of God, who never takes my will, my choice from me, they are mine I have a choice in everything I do and have done so since becoming a Believing Believer. Amen.

I was asked by a Christian what spirit I was following once, and this really wounded me, It is a question I would never ask someone, as I have said it is by your fruits you can be recognised, we must encourage all we meet we must lead people towards the gates of eternal life, not chase them away from it.

It is through my knowledge of God I am able to stand in the gap for my family. Not only my family, all who need prayer, and have asked for it.

**The gap is the distance between the way things are, and the way they should be, I can stand firm strong, tall and straight** and I do so with confidence shunning off the devil's evil attempts to destroy me through my actions or the actions of others.

I was praying with someone once and was told in no uncertain terms 'It is not you I need it is God' there was never a truer word spoken that evening. All the same we must be very careful whom we send away through our ignorance, the messenger maybe an angel sent there by the very one they say they want.

My husband, and I continued with our learning, with each New Year there came new words new ways to do things, and all were considered to be in the line of progress.

I said when I started school I walked home, we had progress with a bus, which incidentally started its run the year my sister started school.

I drove a bus and relinquished it through having a mild heart attack: well this is what I was told. Not for bus drivers Huh?

Too risky and even though I walk with God this doesn't exclude me from being flawed, I am but a mere mortal. I like my handcraft perfect and have achieved this but not myself well not here on earth anyway.

My hubby and I were getting older and this brought along little happenings which I knew in my heart were our lot, they have been in the life cycle of order since 'forever'.

When the next health issue came along we stepped into it like the pros we had become with no allowances for any knock backs.

We stayed focusing on the light of Jesus, we stayed praising God.

My hubby was prescribed insulin for his diabetes as diet was no longer able to control it. Four injections a day, is how it went for several years. As he was of strong mind he learnt very quickly how to use the blood test kits and monitor him self very efficiently.

We had given up the farm work as health and age decided it for us, my hubby pottered about on a piece of land he and the boys had bought, planting pine trees the 'in thing' at the time and sometimes even the pottering seemed to be too much for him.

Things never turn out how we expect or plan somehow funny isn't it. I heard a joke once saying 'if you want to make God laugh tell Him your plans'.

Our plans are certainly, not the same as the Masters are they?

One boy travelled to another country where he eventually decided to stay and make his home, and with further education he has achieved a successful business in a garden architectural profession.

Bringing some landscape designs of his homeland into very much sought after projects.

He has a partner whom we love and a little daughter, his very own family.

May God stay and bless them always.

His father was very proud of both his sons and as he pottered about with his little dog he seemed happy enough.

My hubby began showing signs of further deterioration he was constantly unwell; the prognosis was the last stages of renal failure. We were told his kidneys would cease their function in about twelve months.

One trauma gone two more to follow I was told, I turned 61 nothing too bad there as I recall Eight days later my mother died, she was 82 years young.

I grieved for her passing, and at the same my heart ached for my hubby, both were blows not needed.

With the strength of God who controlled the situation neither he nor I picked up the pity party invitation the devil was shoving under our noses.

We smiled and once again stepped into learning, me without my mother, and my hubby coming to terms with the dialysis treatment in front of him.

My hubby had already lost his parents, his father died six years before his mother, they are both at rest now, at his mothers funeral which was rather an 'occasion in and occasion' for I was acknowledged again.

Do I say Hallelujah?

My hubby asked me if I would speak a eulogy!

My feelings of this clan gathering went beyond the pale, and my going was only for my hubby and his mother, reading the eulogy was only for them and no one else.

I had deliberately been excluded from any of the past family invitations so what was different now?

I had no ill feelings toward his mother, and had visited her a few days before she died, it was at her request for me to see her as she wanted me on my own, hubby drove me there waiting outside while we were together.

We talked about many things, and I was thankful for all she shared, and what she showed me. This was the same as when my sister died, these two dying women warned me of things to happen, and both gave me peace for my future.

God works in mysterious ways.

He is awesome there is no doubt, when he is going to close a door on whatever in life, you can be sure He will have opened another first. The evidence of this is in my walk with Him.

I have deliberated over my next comments and it was in a question from an outsider that I was to receive the answer and I knew what I could write.

One can blame the innocent, and the devil will love this.

Do not in life blame God for the things the devil does to us.

In the same vein God has said 'do not give the devil credit for what I am doing in your life'.

Quite a profound statement do you not think?

It only takes one leader; one voice to deliberate anyone being excluded, from anything, it takes only one instigator.

Judgemental criticism can be very cruel. Being judgemental protects nobody.

I have forgiven the hurt inflicted upon myself and my hubby; when judgements come against another it will only bring disharmony, strife for it is a sin.

There is only one judge, and He is watches from above all the time, and will mete out the same measure to those on judgement day.

I was slightly shocked to hear hubby say 'I cannot forgive this from my own family'. He was kind and gentle to all, but he never forgave face to face the one who stabbed him.

As I have written I forgave, but certainly not forgotten although with time and as other things have come along the memory is dull. It was my hubby and I who were left to pay the price for those who played judge and jury.

We both took a step back, as Jesus did when the people of Nazareth wanted to push him off the cliff, He slipped quietly away.

Life is short and not ours to dally with.

Making judgements doesn't bring harmony.

When two spirits are at logger heads with one another this can cause disharmony, so just slip quietly away.

There will come a day when you can build a bridge for others to Cross over

Peace for my hubby became my main objective in the last few years we had together. I did build the bridge at the right time and yes it was God's time.

I am so grateful to be of God's family this means I don't have to be the judge and jury of those around me.

My hubby and I looked for a miracle to happen in our family, as he lived the last seven months of his life, it never happened, and now of course it is too late.

The girls have gone their own way, and he was not to see or hear from them before he died.

My mother and I always argued, when two people are alike this can happened, with us it was the mother daughter syndrome, we both agreed to disagree.

With this I can not be found guilty of desertion, not for anything; and definitely no petty argument ever separated us for any length of time.

We would get together, when the air was clear and talk over the minor squeamish.

My mother gave birth to me and my sister, we both had food beautiful clothes and in her own way she loved us both although I never ever heard her tell us so.

I remember being told about her own childhood she was the youngest of four and arrived ten years after three boys. Life was hard for them as well as many of the families of that era. My grandfather was a War veteran. If you leave home over a dispute of which you feel justified in never returning, may you realize life is too short, to hold disrespect for your siblings and parents?

A prayer here for all of you, and my two daughters, may you learn 'we do not have to agree on everything which occurs in our lifetime, the damage comes from our mouths and we must always be careful what we say, the words in the air cannot be parcelled up and put back into our mouths.

Sometimes it is the innocent paying the price, once the cast is set, it is too late, value your heritage, and remember your family are to be loved not kicked when down.

Settle breaches before sundown as we are advised to do in the Bible.


***God was wonderful to me for I heard Him say 'forgive them child they know what they did to you and my hubby, what they do not know is how you are reacting'***

My hubby started his peritoneal dialysis treatment he chose this way rather than the haemodialysis for his renal failure; he believed it would give him more freedom. I never did see his reasoning there, but as I wasn't the one receiving it his decision was final.

His renal treatment had arrived to stay; he studiously or diligently whichever word you like did this for seven years right up until the day before he died. It was not until he actually had mastered the, 'to do and not to do' with it that he actually resigned himself to being retired. My heart bleed for him as his life breath was now on loan.

We were to have frequent trips to the dialysis ward at the hospital two hours away, the travelling was a bit of a toll but we both managed.

Each time we went my husband was a witness for God to the nursing staff he came in contact with, as I did also.

The hand of God is very large, soft and gentle and I was to see Him work through me when I did my counselling, with the results of joy in my clients lives, I still reap from this line of work and being voluntary it is always at the right time, from the reaping of God's peace I keep sowing into others, who call on me.

We bought a camper van and had many drives away for we equipped it out with the dialysis gear, we both drove it, only thing my hubby didn't want to get out of the drivers seat.

We had a beautiful time but it had to end. My hubby was now my first priority although at times I knew he wanted to be alone in the house so I would spend time outside or made visits to a client giving him the space he wanted.

In his last year of which he only lived five months I was able to talk to clients on the phone, he said once he liked to hear my voice as it calmed him, blessings.

We both managed for seven years with his dialysis treatment without too many hiccups, it is a treatment to take very seriously as any neglect could mean Peritonitis which we avoided like the plague.

Our son came home for Christmas and it was while he was with us we learnt we had to learn again. It was lovely to see the boys with their father being happy, I know my hubby waited for his daughters to come as well, but this didn't happen he waited right up till until he died for this miracle.

There is nothing I can say here about this, where ever they are though they are still our daughters. Nothing will ever change that.

We had our crunch time for my hubby collapsed at home and was taken post haste into hospital.

The prognosis was Aortic Stenosis, and with his diabetes and renal failure there was little to be done for him surgically in fact he was told he would not come out of intensive care.

Tough, but true maybe the hardest thing about this truth, was the deliverance for it wasn't very gentle. Our son had returned to his home, and waiting for the call to say come back if you can.

The greatest blessing any family can have we were given, my husband for forty seven years and the boy's father was with us at home right up 'till death do us part'.

I was able to love and care for and tend to him, until he became a palliative care patient, but still at home. I caught him several times looking at me and when this happened I felt he wanted to say something, his smile was gentle and sad.

Was he asking me to stop everything to make it go away? Was I too close to read it?

Did Jesus have this same look on his face when he shed his Blood for us on the Cross?

*Matthew 27:46 CEV*

*'Eloi, Eloi, lama sabachtha-ni?' which means 'My God, my God, why have you deserted me'?*

Was this the same situation? The wonderful thing is he did not have to do what had been done by Jesus, take on the worlds sins.

Praise the Lord, but we could not deny it was wind down time for him.

The deterioration in his health was now very noticeable. And the time had come for bridges to be built.

I built the bridge and opened the door telling his siblings the situation and left it to them.

This was the day when my hubby said 'well you are now the head no longer the tail'.

I told him what would happen after it was all over where his family were concerned, and he smiled gently and agreed to the path I had chosen.

Then he prayed a silent word to all who had kicked us both, when we were down.

He was absolutely wonderful when talking about the after, I was not to visit the cemetery also he didn't want a headstone he wanted a rock with a plaque on it, as things have turned out it would have been better to have obeyed.

By this time he was being wheeled from room to room as he didn't have the strength to walk any more, his bed was in the living room with me, and by now his eating was almost nothing, it seemed to be more than he could manage. Yes the last months of his life were very tough as he was in untold pain.

I was to loose a very dear friend a few weeks before my hubby passed away and a few weeks after his passing I was to lose my other best friend. Three special people were taken in the same year, leaving me very bereft, and alone.

Our second boy flew back to be with his father the week before he died to give his support to his brother and me for the end was nigh. A family not totally complete never mind we four enjoyed each other's company, and I was able to leave the men together and do things which I had been leaving undone.

There was one thing we never ever said, and this was he would get well, it would have been a lie which would have been cruel to him, and anyone else. We were living in the truth and believe me it is easy to be this way. There was peace and happiness in the house, and each one of our hearts.

Three evenings before he died he had a desire to listen to his favourite music, so I was sitting in his wheelchair beside him, all night listening to music while he held my hand and reminisced; it was rather special, and comes to my mind when I hear any of the music again. There are things in life we will always remember they may not be of importance as such, but they will stay with you.

Two mornings later at 6 o'clock, my hubby told me

He was going to stop his dialysis treatment, and then he looked straight at me and said 'I am holding on for you'.

Excuse me! Was this a joke?

I answered, 'Darling you will be able to see me better from up there than down here.'

It was here I remembered the gentle smile he had given to me a short while ago, and realised he wasn't asking me to stop or change anything he was asking permission to 'float away'

He had been waiting for the permission of release for he suddenly relaxed, and I knew the acceptable time of God had finally crept upon us.

My hubby had accepted with my words his release from us; as well he had accepted the words of Jesus

### *Matthew 20:22 CEV*

### *'Are you able to drink from the cup that I must soon drink from'?*

My hubby knew Jesus had drunk from the cup. He knew he was forgiven of all his sins, he was ready for God to take him on the trip to a new mansion, and he was going there to wait for my calling to come home to be with him again.

I called out to our boy, who called the other and his wife ; they both arrived looking as if they had been sleeping in their clothes waiting for the call.

My hubby was in intense pain, which showed on his face he had a son on each side of him and as they laid him back on his pillows half in my arms he looked up at the boys with recognition and said their names and, ' what a bloody performance' and within a couple of breaths he 'floated away' peacefully to be in the arms of his maker.

What a beautiful memory of departing from this world we are able to share with you.

The man I had known for fifty years and been married to for forty seven was at last in the care of someone, who would see he rested without pain.

The time I had with my best friend, a husband, a protector and a man who would always look to satisfy me before himself had gone from the earth, he was the father of four children and a loving grandfather to his grandchildren and they knew he loved them dearly.

He was now in the safest place he could be.

Through the following days my sons shielded me as my hubby would have done. I just wanted to recall all he had told me in the last few days when we were alone together.

Things like 'you are not to worry

'You will be alright' and 'you are strong.'

He knew my strength in the Lord, maybe he didn't know or believe but in the natural it was he, who also kept me strong. I was breaking in half with the pain of loosing him.

I was only strong when I was walking in the strength of the Lord, and when I had my man near.

What a test in front of me.

I suddenly realised I was the matriarch of a family, just as my mother had been before me. The boys brought everything together the arranging what their father had planned for his funeral.

Like who he wanted for his pall bearers, the music, and where he wanted to be buried, which was with my parents, my sister and her husband. He wanted this for me, he had said. In his death he still wanted to satisfy me. God bless his memory.

He had taught me all the things he knew I would need after he had gone, like the hedge trimmer, how to drive the ride on mower, how to hammer nails in my bird cages without hitting my thumbs.

The learning, I had from him in his last months was phenomenal, there wasn't a thing left out, except he would not teach me how to use the power-saw. He refused point blank.

We had talked about if it was me that floated away first, and so I taught him cooking, and how to use the washing machine things he would have to know. And all the things a woman uses around the house.

We were together people. We were as one.

When a partner dies there are such a lot of adjustments, one has to make, I eventually made them it was not easy when I went into town I would still rush home forgetting there was no one there to help or rush in and say 'hello I am home, did you miss me?'

He was remembered at his funeral by the many who had met and liked him. He was there so would know.

There is something for all to remember if you have been in any of the situations mentioned in this book please keep yourself in reality things happen whether we have created them or not, it doesn't matter stay real. We all know my husband lived his last months on borrowed time, and I was able to prepare each one for the inevitable, to keep him happy and the boys for their initial grief, which I knew would be silent and deep within, the grandchildren to know he was going to be safe, but the downside, was I never prepared myself.

This is what I meant stay real; I was part of it not apart from it.

My story concludes

With one becoming two, who both knew when they met they had been given a love to share a love they could build their live together on.

I write with this same love the attributes of a man who was a gentleman through and through.

A man who came to know his maker, was happy to 'float away' to be with him.

He was chosen for me, and will now be a memory we were as one heart given to each other to love and cherish fifty years ago all from the heart of God.

My hubby had a love for his family and the ability to see each one as they truly were. He loved his boys with a love only a father can have.

He loved his daughters as well, and although I believe they failed their father, it is not for me to judge their reasons; I pray they are at peace with their actions for they failed themselves more.

My hubby had a sense of humour, which never wavered no matter how much pain was thrown at him, and he never complained too much for he spoke about his illness with intelligence and eventually acceptance.

He had a cheeky grin which his family would look for.

He had a fighting Spirit

And this rubbed off on to others.

He had twinkling eyes which I miss.

He was a hard worker.

As well as his children he had a great love for his little dog Timothy, who has now gone to be with him, at the age of eleven.

I have released you sweetheart.

And I now close the door.

Please rest in peace.

Amen.